LETTERS FROM AIX-EN-PROVENCE 1960-61

A young Fulbright scholar's adventures in France & abroad

WARREN ZITLAU

© Warren Zitlau 2021

All rights reserved. No part of this publication may be reproduced, distributed, or transmitted in any form or by any means, including photocopying, recording, or other electronic or mechanical methods, without the prior written permission of the publisher, except in the case of brief quotations embodied in critical reviews and certain other noncommercial uses permitted by copyright law.

Printed in the United States of America

ISBN: 978-1-7364977-0-8 (Paperback)
ISBN: 978-1-7364977-1-5 (Hardcover)

First Edition
10   9   8   7   6   5   4   3   2   1

In Memory

Barbara Ann Snow Zitlau
(1938-2017)

Her children rise up and call her blessed
– Prov. 31:28a

Table of Contents

Introduction vii
The Voyage Over 1
First Stop: Paris 7
On to Aix! 41
    Cannes 69
    Spain 107
    Morocco 133
    Return to France via Spain 143
    Côte d'Azur 175
    Italy 219
    Switzerland 267
Back to Paris 293
United Kingdom 303
Goodbye to France 321

Introduction

My mother, Barbara Ann Snow, received a Fulbright Scholarship to study in Aix-en-Provence, France in 1960-61. It was one of the defining moments of her life.

Shortly after her death in 2017, I read through the following letters she wrote to her beloved parents, Warren and Rachel Snow. I am now 30 years *older* than my mother was when she mailed these letters and postcards back home from France, Spain, Morocco, Italy, Switzerland, and Great Britain.

Seeing my mother as a single, 23 year old navigating the world has been wonderful. She is the same woman I recognize as my mom, with a love of life, food, art, history, cultures, language, and people. Some of her hopes and dreams are new to me, such as her desire to go to graduate school, and I have enjoyed reading her comments about dating and her French boyfriend.

I admire her determination to travel in the days before easy international phone calls, email, instant access to maps and directions on a smartphone, online reviews, automatic hotel check-in, and ATMs. Courage and effort were required to experience foreign countries.

The conflicting realities of a young woman raised in the '40s and '50s are evident. Barbara uses the words "colored" and "non-colored" to refer to people in a completely descriptive way, yet acknowledges that society, and particularly the church, has fostered racial prejudice. Raised in a traditional mainstream Protestant church, she had little positive understanding of anything Catholic, yet had a painting of the Madonna and Child in her childhood bedroom; took efforts to have a medal blessed by the Pope sent to her neighbor in Delaware; and was avidly pro-Kennedy. Her senior thesis was on the educational theories of Fénelon, the 17th century French priest and royal tutor.

In the midst of French political uncertainties regarding Algerian independence, the US-Russia space race and cold war, and an American presidential election, the focus of her letters remains on personal relationships, adapting to French culture and bureaucracy, living on a stipend, and planning her future. She remained a Francophile her entire life.

The following article is from the student newspaper, *The Review*, at the University of Delaware regarding her Fulbright scholarship—in the days before spell check.

Delaware Review

Vol. 83   No. 24   Newark, Delaware   April 22, 1960

◆ NEWARK, DELAWARE

Spring Spots "Circus Capers"

Barbara Snow Wins Fullbright Scholarship

French Student To Study in Aix

First Stop: Paris

By ERNIE LEVY

Barbara Snow, senior French major has recently been awarded a Fullbright Scholarship to France. The scholarship will enable Barbara to study abroad on an all-expenses-paid basis for the duration of one school year.

The masters' degree in French language and literature will be sought by the award winner. She will pursue her studies at the University of Aix-Marseilles in Aix, near the French Riviera.

Barbara received her scholarship through the Fullbright Act as given by the government for the purpose of furthering better international relations. Two people per state are accorded the award.

The Phi Beta Kappa student will disembark in mid-Sept. She does not yet know the name of her ship. Barbara will sail directly for Paris where she will undergo a three week orientation season. There different facets of the French government will be discussed along with information concerning the American Embassy.

NO TESTS

Requirements for the Fullbright are numerous although no scholastic tests are administ- (Continued on Page 12)

BARBARA SNOW, senior receives a Fullbright Scholarship to France.

JOHNNIE AUSTIN'S orchestra will be featured in tomorrow's Student Center Dance from 8 p.m. to 12 midnight. This will be the final activity of the Spring Weekend which features The Campus Chest Carnival in Carpenter Field House tonight.

Society Of Civil Engineers Holds Convention on Campus

The university will host the 22nd annual regional convention of student chapters of the American Society of Civil Engineers, on Monday, sponsored jointly by the Central Pennsylvania, Delaware, Lehigh Valley and Philadelphia sections of the society.

Participating schools include Bucknell, Delaware, Drexel, Lafayette, Lehigh, Penn State, Princeton, Swarthmore and Villanova. Each school will present a technical paper for judging. Civil Engineering students at Delaware will preside over the various meetings.

A feature will be a luncheon at 1 p.m. in the Student Center. Speaker will be Dr. Harold B. Gotaas, professor of engineering and dean of the Technological Institute at Northwestern University. His scheduled topic is "Civil Engineering Education for the Future." Jacob Feldman, of Wilmington, vice president of the campus chapter, will preside.

Registration will be in Mitchell Hall at 8 a.m., followed by the first general session at 10. The opening address will be given by Melvin F. Wood, chief engineer of the DuPont Company. (Continued on Page 3)

Lowden and Homen Elected to O.D.K., National Honor Group

Graham Lowden, junior, and Carl-Olaf Homen, special student, were recently selected as members of Omicron Delta Kappa, national leadership honor society.

Graham, a member of Kappa Alpha social fraternity, is treasurer of the junior class, junior representative to the Inter fraternity council, junior representative to the Student Government Association and a member of the junior class Executive Committee. He is also a member of Scabbard and Blade and Chairman of the WDA Standards Committee. He is a member of the intra-

mural volleyball, handball and badminton teams.

Carl, a special student from Finland, comes here for the past term from the University of Helsinki. Carl is studying at this university.
(Continued on Page 12)

Ladies Receive Silver Charms; Dance on Roof

Whirl and Sway To Austin Music

Johnny Austin and his band will play as students whirl and sway at the annual Spring Dance tomorrow night from 8 p.m. until 12 midnight.

Via colorful streamers, gay posters and helium-filled balloons, the Dover Room will be transformed into an atmosphere fit for "Circus Capers," which is the theme for the entire weekend.

In keeping with a carnival atmosphere, the band will play from a center ring on the dance floor. Other fints for the dance include a sterling silver charm which is being given as a favor to each young lady, and a cabaret on the roof top, bedecked with streamers, posters, and a circus tent. Refreshments are also being featured 'neath the stars.

Music will be piped to the cabaret so that all may enjoy the Austin sound. The Austin band, known for its recent work at many schools in the area, also appeared at the Sunnybrook Ballroom in Pottstown, Pa.

Dress for the dance is semiformal. Tickets which have been on sale at the Student Center for two weeks, are still available if purchased today. The price is three dollars per couple.

Also appearing will be the renowned "Miss X." End your weekend with Amusement à la Austin.

Tassel Taps Junior Women Showing Service, Leadership

Tassel, the senior women's honor society on campus, recently tapped six junior women for membership. Chosen were Annette Adams, Lynn Beam, Pat Craven, Sandy Schwab, Ellen Tanfani and Tonya Heesen.

At 6 a.m. on April 12, the six were awakened in the traditional tapping ceremony. The official tapping then took place at 9 a.m. in front of the library. New members were initiated at 4 p.m. and then attended a dinner in their honor at the Glasgow Arms. Guests at the dinner included the six senior members of Tassel, Dean Collins, Dean Ayres and Mrs Arthur Dunlap, sponsors.

Those tapped were chosen on the basis of their scholarship, leadership, and service to the university, and are engaged in a variety of campus activities. Annette Adams, a biology major and member of Tri-Beta, is head of house at Newcastle (Continued on Page 12)

Carl-Olaf Homen

Graham Lowden

TASSEL TAPS — Tassel initiates six junior women. This organization has recently become a member of Mortar Board, the national honorary society.

The following letters and postcards are addressed to Barbara's parents.

Rachel Katherine Heltzel (1908-1990)
Warren Ramon Snow (1908-1983)
Of Bridgewater, Virginia.
The Snow family lived in Wilmington, Delaware
from 1943 – 1969.

The Voyage Over

Photograph of bearer

Renewal, extensions, amendments, limitations, and restrictions

THIS PASSPORT IS NOT VALID FOR TRAVEL TO OR IN COMMUNIST CONTROLLED PORTIONS OF

    CHINA
    KOREA
    VIET-NAM

OR TO OR IN

    ALBANIA

IMM. & NATZ. SERVICE
NEW YORK, N.Y. 32
ADMITTED
JUL 31 1961

Visas

Le Titulaire du présent Visas devra solliciter la délivrance d'une "Carte de Séjour" dans les huit jours qui suivront son entrée en territoire français.

Visa d'ETUDIANT

CONSULAT DE FRANCE A TANGER

Nom : SNOW
Prénoms : Barbara Ann
1. Numéro du Visa : 170/1960
2. Genre de Visa : Long séjour
3. Date de délivrance : 7 septembre 1960
4. Date d'expiration : 6 novembre 1961
5. Nombre d'entrées autorisées : UNE
6. Durée autorisée de chaque séjour : UN AN

Sept. 24 [1960]

Dear Mother & Daddy –

I am having a fabulous time. I have never met such delightful people before, especially the boys. There are 75 Fulbrights on board. Also there are 24 Marshal Scholars who are going to England.

My roommate is very nice. We enjoyed the send-off they gave us in New York very much. My only regret was having to say good-bye to you.

One of the families did not get off in time! A tug boat came out to get them.

The boat is really swaying now. They have put up extra ropes to hang on to in the dining room area. I have rented a deck chair because the deck is the best place to stay. At 11:00 in the morning, soup is served and at 4:00 in the afternoon, we have tea. There is always something to do. Yesterday a group of us had a round of singing – everything from Christmas carols to folk songs.

Thursday night I danced until 2:00 am, but last night many of the kids weren't feeling so well. I have been most fortunate so far. I had a headache yesterday after going to the movies, but it left before long.

Thank you so much for the beautiful flowers – 12 large mums (6 yellow + 6 white). I have written a postcard to Aunt Ruby and Uncle Ike[1], Grandmother[2], Glady[3], Roberta[4], and Mr. Briggs.

If it is too windy Monday, the boat won't land at Cherbourg. Instead, a tender boat will come out to get us. I'm beginning to wonder how that will be accomplished.

The waiter for my table is a very nice "old chap". The food has been delicious. I eat at 9:00, 1:30, and 7:45.

It is a bit difficult to write while swaying back and forth. I will write again when I get to Paris.

Love,
Barb

---

1 Ruby Elizabeth Heltzel Riddleberger (1905-1987) and Hensel Dorsey Riddleberger (1894-1969).

2 Annie Frances Hale Snow (1877-1963).

3 A classmate at the University of Delaware.

4 Roberta Davis Stephenson (1938-2016), classmate at Mount Pleasant High School in Wilmington, DE and roommate at the University of Delaware.

From Travel Log:

9/21-9/26 *Queen Elizabeth*

9/26 – arrived at Cherbourg by tender – took the boat train to Paris (4 hours) – passed thru Caen and saw the beautiful fields of Normandy.
-met by Fulbright representatives
-went to Cité Universitaire Fondation des Etats Unis

September 27

Dear Mother and Dad,

I have finally made it to Paris! I've done so many things that I don't know where to start telling about them.

First of all, the boat trip was delightful. As I told you before, I was very much impressed by the kids. I danced practically every night. I met a terrific boy. He is starting to study law at Oxford. He is a Marshal scholar. He graduated from Dartmouth. We have each other's addresses, but I'm afraid I'll never see him again. There was a fire on the ship last evening. Some of the lights went off.

A tender boat came along side of the *Queen Elizabeth* and took us to Cherbourg. It was so sad to leave the ship and our new friends. The train ride from Cherbourg to Paris took about 4 hours. That part of the country is very lovely. Many times it looks just like the Valley[5] except the architecture of the buildings is much different.

---

5 The Shenandoah Valley of Virginia.

This place where I'm staying in Paris (The United States House) is not too great, but at least it has hot and cold running water. Today we were given our checks - 894.80 NF[6]. I suppose that's close to $178. The committee has done very little to help us. First we had to find the correct bank. Six of us started out on the metro (subway). I must say the metro is very well organized, and we were most pleased with our success. We had to take three different trains. I decided to bring my trunk here because I need so many things. You should have seen the suitcases and trunks some kids brought!

With all this running around, I finally ended up with my roommate. The US ambassador is giving a reception for us Friday night. We have a sightseeing tour tomorrow.... I would be most disheartened if I had to stay here. I wish I was going to Aix tomorrow.

Thanks for your letter. It was so nice to get it with my check this morning.

Love,
Barb

---

6   New Francs. The French currency was revalued in 1960.

Travel Log:

9/27 – saw Place Opéra, rue de la Paix; Place Vendôme. saw about luggage at Gare St. Lazare, had interviews at the Sorbonne

9/28 – bus tour of important sights. Saw Leningrad Orchestra at Palais de Chaillot, walked down to the Eiffel Tower

9/29 – visited Panthéon – saw graves of Voltaire, Rousseau, Hugo, Zola, etc. Saw play - *L'Aigle à deux têtes* by Jean Cocteau at Théâtre Sarah Bernhardt

My trunk arrived in good condition.

September 30

Dear Mother and Dad,

Well, I'm still navigating. I like my courses very much. They are given at the Sorbonne. The French call their bathrooms water closets (W.C.). Yesterday, I went to the WC at the Sorbonne and was horrified! It is used by both sexes. I decided I would have to be deathly ill before I used anything like that!

The other day, my roommate and I took the metro (subway) back to the U.S. house. You can imagine the look on our faces when the train didn't stop at our stop (Cité Universitaire). It went straight through and we ended up 8 stops later, somewhere in the suburbs of Paris. Fortunately, the officials were very nice and we found a train back. All in all, I have had much success riding the metros. They are so well organized.

Now for the brighter side - we saw all the major points of interest on our bus tour. Yesterday, I saw the Pantheon where many great French men are buried such as Voltaire, Rousseau, Victor Hugo, Émile Zola, etc. The Luxembourg Gardens are really beautiful. Last night, I saw a play by Jean Cocteau of the Académie Française. Jay had studied it, so I was able to understand much of it.

Tonight, we are going to a reception given by the U.S. ambassador then to the Comédie-Française to see Molière's play *Le Bourgeois gentilhomme*. I suggested to one of my teachers that we visit Versailles - she thought it was a good idea.

I met two perfectly delightful girls who are also going to Aix. One is from Richmond, Virginia and the other is from Chattanooga, Tennessee. Maggie is staying in Paris. Write soon.

Love, Barb

I was shocked to hear about Margie.[7] Now I can't see the wedding.

---

7 Margie Evans, a neighbor and childhood friend.

October 1

Dear Mother & Dad,

Thank you so much for your letters. I always get a lump in my throat when I read them, but I still enjoy them. I miss you a lot, also my car, friends, and Pepsi.

I think I am particularly anxious to get news from you because I <u>do not like</u> Paris. Today the hot water went off and we have been cold since we got here. I feel so sorry for the poor kids who must day. The electricity is 220 so no one has been able to iron.

We have had some great times! The girls I go around with are just delightful. Today we visited the Luxembourg Gardens again and then walked down to the Seine. Notre Dame is a marvel, and when you climb up the tower, you can see across the entire city. However, I was much more impressed with the beautiful little chapel called Sainte-Chapelle. There are raised gold fleur-de-lis all over the walls and the stained windows are so beautiful and in such good taste.

The reception at the American Embassy was very nice. They served champagne and sandwiches.

I met the French novelist, M. Botour[8], who visited the University [of Delaware] last spring. In fact, he is going to give a lecture for the Fulbrights at the Sorbonne. After the reception, my roommate and I went to see Molière's play *Bourgeois gentilhomme*. I really enjoyed it.

Tomorrow we are going to the Louvre and then at night to see *Carmen* at the opera. I'm really becoming an old hand at using the metro. I have located the address where your office friend will be staying, Daddy, so I will certainly try to see her.

If it is a nice day Monday, our French teacher is going to take us to Versailles.

We often eat at the International House at the Cité Universitaire. The food is not too bad. At least you feel as though you're getting something substantial. I have bought several cokes - They are about 14¢. Please write soon.

Love, Barb

---

8 Michel Marie François Butor (1926-2016).

Travel Log:

10/1 walked around Luxembourg Gardens and down Bld. St. Michel – saw Notre Dame and climbed tower – then saw Sainte-Chapelle* (magnifique)

10/2 visited Louvre – saw the *Winged Victory of Samothrace* – *Mona Lisa* (was smaller than I had expected), Raphael's *La Jardiniere* – series of Marie de Medici by Reubens, [da Vinci's] *The Virgin and Child with St. Anne*. Saw Arc de Triomphe du Carousel (pink marble). After snack at café we went to the l'Opéra and saw *Carmen*. Real horses on stage – beautiful building. Opéra was founded by Louis XIV in 1669, this building was built around 1870.

10/3 met M. Ruff from Aix – charming. Visited Versailles – beautiful formal gardens – chapel (white and gold), Opéra (blue and gold) – apartments of M. Antoinette and the king – the opera was dazzling. Came home alone on metro.

10/4 – classes – lecture on religious aspects in France. Saw movie at night *Hiroshima, mon amour* – very subtle

10/5 Lecture - how to take notes – after class went with Alec to his room near St. Germain des Pres. Spoke with Frenchmen - then to dinner at the *Rest des Beaux Arts* (delicious food), sat at Jean Paul Sartre's Café, *Les Deux Margots* and drank French beer. Pastry party for Cricket.[9]

---

9 Dr. Elsie Minter from Virginia (1925-2003). The origin of the name "Cricket" is never disclosed. In a telephone conference with Elsie Minter's son, he stated that her father gave her the nickname Cricket because, as a little girl, she hopped around everywhere.

October 6

Dear Mother and Daddy,

Thanks so much for the letter. I really miss you both. I think Margie's picture is very cute. I wrote her, Kathy, and their parents[10] telling them how sad I am that I won't be there. Kathy wrote that even Dr. Christie[11] would be there!!

Yes, I have the same roommate that I had on the boat. She is a lovely girl. All my best friends over here seem to be from the South except Maggie. Cathie Oliver is from Charleston, South Carolina. Two girls are from Richmond. One of the girls going to Aix is from Tennessee. I have met a very nice boy who is from Columbia, South Carolina. He went to Sewanee or another name is the College of the South. He also was awarded a Wilson scholarship and hopes to study at Harvard next year. This year, he will be at Dijon.

---

10 The Evans family were neighbors and the 2 daughters, Kathy and Margie, were good friends of Barbara.

11 Dr. Rev. John W. Christie (1883-1974). Pastor of Westminster Presbyterian Church in Wilmington, DE (1931-1956).

I am in need of your assistance. Most of the kids brought their diplomas and birth certificates. My birth certificate is on the second shelf of the open part of my bookcase. The diploma is on the first shelf in the enclosed part. Daddy, could you get a photostatic copy of the diploma? I would like to have them as soon as possible. Monday, I met M. Ruff, the Fulbright advisor at Aix. He is a lovely man and gave us his address. I think I will be in good hands if I can just get there!! The plan now is to leave the 19th for Aix. Do not worry about my address. I will always eventually get my mail if sent in care of the Fulbright Commission. I will send my permanent address just as soon as I can get it, if that day ever comes. I want so much just to get settled and have a little place of my own. Last night, some of us wrote a letter to a hotel asking for a room so we could at least have some place to go when we arrived.

Please do send all of the news you can about the US and Wilmington. The French newspapers say very little about us. I get the feeling that some of them don't particularly care for us. There are many colored people over here from Algeria. It is nothing to walk down the street and see mixed couples. A few of the colored boys have tried to pick up girls, but they've had no success, especially with the Southern girls.

Oh, yes! I've been trying out my French on the natives. We eat lunch at a different café almost every day. When we eat here at the cafeteria, we still have to speak French if we want to converse with any of the other students. It is rather rough! Especially when most things are so disorganized. Yet you get a great sense of satisfaction when you can order a meal or go into a pharmacy and come out with toothpaste and the equivalent to Kleenex. Today, I went to the American embassy to get my voting papers signed by a notary public. It is very nice with blue velvet carpet on the stairs. I found an American restaurant there and Lois and I had a chocolate sundae. We were so delighted to have paper napkins! Very few restaurants serve any kind of napkins.

Did I tell you that we went to Versailles? It is really a marvelous place. If the weather is nice, we are going back Saturday. Sunday, we are going to see *Faust* at the opera. I wish I knew more about the opera. I enjoyed *Carmen*, but I think I still prefer plays.

I've heard from Kathy, Mrs. Evans, Gladys, Roberta, Mrs. Stephenson, and Al. You can't imagine how much I appreciate all of your letters! Things have settled down some this week and I am enjoying it much more than last. Besides the hot water is now on. (I think it was off for 4 days). Tell everyone "hello" from me and write soon.

Love,
Barby

PS – You can use either address.

Travel Log:

10/6 – went to Commission met Mr. Watson. Went to American Embassy about voting - ate chocolate sundae in the American Rest. Went to Palais Royal – Tuileries – Museum of Impressionist Painting (Monet, Manet, Van Gogh, Cézanne, Renoir, Degas, etc.). I liked best Renoir's *Le Moulin de la Galette*; Degas - *La Classe de danse*.

10/7 – went to Embassy, then to Palais Royal – walked around shops and gardens and bought 2 tickets to Comédie Française (*Electra*) by Jean Giraudoux. Lecture at the Sorbonne, lunch at Rest. Parthénon – ate gâteau napoléon. Reception at Hôtel des Deux Mondes (22 Ave. L'Opéra). Ate dinner with Alec & Allison – then saw play (very good and Charlton Heston was there).

10/8 went to Versailles – walked around gardens down to the grand canal….went with Alec to Chinese restaurant – delicious food (egg roll, noodles with chicken – lychee), then to L'Abbaye (a Fr. Beatnik nightclub – Gordon Heath and

Lee Payant[12]), snapped fingers, few lights, French & English folk songs. Also went to church at St. Germain des Prés. St. Denis = Patron Saint of Paris – picked up his head and walked to Saint-Denis.

10/9 Sunday church service at the German House – very good. Ate dinner at Hotel Louvre with Cathie and Cricket – saw Greek and Roman statues at the Louvre went to *Faust* at the Opera, enjoyed ballet Act III.

---

12 Heath and Payant ran the nightclub from 1949-1976.

October 10

Dear Mother and Daddy,

There are so many things to tell you that I don't know where to start. Friday night, I went to the reception given by the Fulbright Commission. It was the best one yet. I was delighted to find Monique Morelec there. She was the French Fulbright student at [the University of] Delaware last year. We had a nice long chat. Then I met the French Fulbright student who was at Delaware three years ago. She was the one who gave us some French magazines. Then I met Shirley Gross who is from Delaware and got a Fulbright 3 years ago. The four of us had a kind of Delaware reunion in Paris.

Then after having some supper, Alec, another girl, and I went to the Comédie française and saw Jean Giraudoux's play *Electra*. It was very good and guess what? - Charlton Heston was there with his wife!! He is quite good-looking. He was taking down notes all evening.

Saturday we went again to Versailles. This time we toured the gardens and walked over to the Hameau. That's the little village that Marie Antoinette built where she could be alone in nature and "play at keeping house". The gardens are beautiful. This little village has thatched roofs on quaint little houses, little footbridges, a big goldfish pond, weeping willows, a Temple of Love, etc. It was very rustic and romantic. Lois and I thought it was the nicest time we had so far. We also took a tour through the large rooms in the castle and saw the Hall of Mirrors. I was really thrilled to find a painting of Fénelon!

Saturday night Alec and I went to a Chinese restaurant; the food was much better than that I had at Philadelphia. And we went to a little nightclub called l'Abbaye. The people snapped their fingers instead of clapping. A white man and a dark man sang and played guitars. Half of their songs were American folk songs or spirituals, and the other half were French songs.

Yesterday, Cathie, Cricket, and I ate Sunday dinner together and went to the Louvre. This time we saw the *Venus de Milo* and the Greek & Roman statues. I didn't enjoy these as much as the paintings. Besides, none of the men statues have on much clothing and the women aren't much better. Then we had tea and went to the opera – saw *Faust*. It was very good - although I find it extremely difficult to understand French when it is being sung. One of the girls told me the story of

Faust before I went. There was also a little ballet in one of the acts so I feel as though I've had enough of that kind of cultural activity for a while. I really enjoyed the plays more!

Today our teacher took us out to Saint Denis. This is a town outside Paris. It is also one of the oldest French churches. Most of the Kings are buried there. A guide showed us all the tombs. However, during the revolution most of the bodies were removed so I doubt there was much left! It was very cold in the church and the guide spoke very poorly so we weren't impressed although the building itself was rather nice.

Some of us going to Aix have made reservations with a hotel in Aix, Hotel de Provence, Rue Espariat Aix-en-Provence. I suppose after the 18th, you can write me there until I find a permanent place. I paid for the rest of my room here today.

I plan to get in touch with Miss Corleto this week. I am hoping she will bring back 2 rolls of film for me. You do what you like with them. The weather has been miserable so they probably aren't all good. There should be some nice pictures of the Statue of Liberty and the Luxembourg Gardens. Sunday I went to a Protestant church service at the German House. The service was almost identical to ours. It seems very strange to say the Lord's prayer, repeat the Apostles' Creed, and sing familiar hymns in French. The chaplain was very good so I was at least able to understand the sermon.

No one has written in their last four days and I'm getting quite angry!! If they don't think anymore of me than that, I may just forget them. Of course, I think you have been doing very well, and I certainly do appreciate hearing from you.

Love,
Barby

Travel Log:

10/10 - Lecture by Mme Léon – compared French spoken by A. Camus, B. Bardot, Gen. de Gaulle. Afternoon trip to Saint Denis where most of the kings are buried (lovely windows). Met Alec at *Le Deux Magots* – ate at restaurant on Boulevard St. Michel, then went to Montmartre. Climbed steps up to Sacré-Couer and looked out over Paris**. Then went to Pigalle thru red light district saw the Moulin Rouge.

10/11 – wonderful lecture on the European market by M. Jean François-Poncet (in English). Ate with Alec at Rest. on St. Michel. After class walked down to Seine bookstalls with Lois near Notre Dame. I bought a book about Fénelon. Then over to Louvre. At department store bought leather gloves and sortilège for mother. Home in rush hour (almost smashed to death). Listened to English station on radio.

10/12 – bought Daddy's tie. At night went to Opéra-Comique and saw *La Bohème* (very good). Made phone call to Anne Corleto[13] – Hotel Rafael.

10/13 – Took presents and film over to Anne Corleto Hotel Rafael – ate breakfast and had nice chat with her. Afternoon, class went to Châteaux de Vincennes - saw chapel and dungeon where Diderot and Mirabeau were imprisoned – walked around with Alec – went to Nixon-Kennedy debate filmed by American Cultural Service. Walked with Alec down to Seine & Notre Dame*** - over to Les Halles.

---

13 Presumably Anne X. Corleto (1921-1967). She was a secretary in DuPont's textile fibers department.

October 14

Dear Mother and Daddy,

At least while I'm living over here, I have a lot of news to tell you. Yesterday, I went to Miss Corleto's room at the Hotel Rafael. She was very nice. We had breakfast in her room and a very lovely time. She is bringing home 2 rolls of film and a little present for each of you. I'm sorry I couldn't send bigger presents, but thought I had better watch my money; however, I did think you both should have something from Paris. Mother, I bought your present at a large department store across the street from the Louvre. Also near the Palais Royale where the Comedie française presents its plays.

Daddy, your present comes from the Boulevard St. Michel about two blocks from the Sorbonne. Also near the Seine. The Hotel Rafael is really quite lovely. If you should decide to come to France you might ask Ms. Corleto about the prices. Of course, they may be too high.

We had a very fine lecture one morning about the European market. I wish you could have been here Daddy because you certainly know much more about it then I do. At any rate, he said it was definitely here to stay and that many American businessmen have been investing in it.

One day after class Lois and I walked down to the book stalls along the Seine. I was right across from Notre Dame when I saw a book about Fénelon. Everything seemed so romantic that I bought it! It was only 3 francs.

Sometimes we get Radio Luxembourg on my radio. It is usually in English. One night they played almost all the top American tunes. We really enjoyed it. Last night a gang of us saw the second Nixon-Kennedy debate. The American Cultural Service filmed it and brought it over. I really did enjoy it!!

Sunday night we saw *La Bohème* by Puccini. It was translated into French. This time we went to the Opéra comique. I enjoyed this the most. It was not as much a spectacular, but it was more personal. I wish I had my opera book here with me, but don't send it because I doubt that there will be any operas in Aix.

Last night Alec and I walked down along the Seine (how romantic!) and then over to Les Halles. This is where all the fresh produce is brought. We went by one large block where all kinds of meat were hanging. You should have seen some of the large slabs of meat. We also saw whole pigs. Then we ate some onion soup and came home.

If it sounds like I am having a great time, I am. I am really going to miss all of my friends that I've made in Paris. It seems so cruel to keep having to lose such great friends; however, some of us plan to visit each other and maybe even travel together. As I wrote before, I have a hotel reservation in Aix. Yesterday we bought our tickets and made arrangements for baggage. I also wrote to Mme Lisle. She will give us a list of available rooms when we arrive.

Alec is quite the socialite from Columbia, so I've found out. I like him, but I wouldn't be caught dead living in that kind of society. Lois is from Georgia. She says that her family is not quite in the elite circles, but that this emphasis on family name and land is quite prominent in the South. Alec comes from two of the oldest families in Columbia and goes to many of the debutante balls.

Our French teacher really astonished us yesterday by saying one great fault in the US is that we place too much emphasis on religion. Many French people only go to church three times during their lives: baptism, marriage, and funeral. She also said that when her husband taught last year in the US, he told the kids he didn't believe in God. She thinks it was just terrible that the kids were so surprised and horrified. I was rather horrified myself to hear her talk like that.

Tomorrow we are going on a bus trip sponsored by our teachers. Sunday night we have tickets to see Paul Claudel's play *Christophe Colomb*. Time to start packing again-This should be great fun (ha!). Hope you're both well and happy --- and miss me!

Love, Barb

Travel Log:

10/14 – Classes. Saw Musée de Cluny, many medieval relics – bought Michelin guide of Côte D'Azur. Ate dinner with Cathie, Lois, and Cricket – wrote letters and rested.

10/15 day trip – Chantilly north of Paris. Lovely old château, smaller than Versailles. Beautiful landscaping. At Senlis visited the church and had great fun climbing the towers and walks. Visited the place were Rousseau spent his last days & was originally buried. Saw movie on the Champs-Élysées.

At Senlis – met an old Fr. man who said the German soldiers were much better than the Italian.

10/16 – went with Cricket, Cathie, and Judy to Chartres. The cathedral is the most beautiful and awe-inspiring church I have ever seen – tall towers, arches, beautiful windows – altar to the Black Virgin. Also went to Musée, had lunch and tea – saw mass – choir boys chanting and organ played – also baptism and assembly for a pilgrimage. Sunday night saw Claudel's play *Christophe Colomb*. – very good, modern, pantomime, symbolical. Met M.F. Toinet[14] at Théâtre l'Odéon completely by chance.

10/17 – picked up check at Commission and cashed it. Picked up laissez-passer at Louvre with Lois, walked around Paris. Had tea with M.F. and family. She showed me around St. Germain des Prés – saw part of the original old wall of Paris. Place where guillotine was invented. At night, birthday party for Mimi and Rob – adjourned to nearby café and sang and danced.

....
14 Presumably Marie-France Toinet (1942-1995).

October 18

Dear Mother and Daddy,

Well here I am spending my last night in gay Paris! The time really flew after the first few days. I actually think I will miss it quite a bit. After much arranging and several crises, I think I'm all ready. The trunk is at the station - in fact, I think it may have left on the 9:00 train. The bus trip Saturday was very nice. We saw a lovely château called Chantilly. We visited the church at Senlis and we climbed all over it - even up to the steeple. Also saw another Château de Chalais. On the way back, we passed by the place where Rousseau spent his last days and was originally buried.

Saturday night, Lois and I went to a movie near the Champs-Élysées called *Never on Sunday* (*Jamais le dimanche*). Greek and English were spoken with French subtitles. Also saw an old Bugs Bunny cartoon with French subtitles. When Bugs Bunny says, "What's up, Doc," the French translation is "Alors, Vieux".

Sunday, Cathie, Cricket, and I went to Chartrés. It took about an hour to get there, but it was well worth it. The cathedral is the most beautiful and magnificent church I have ever seen. The windows are lovely and the arches are so high that you get a kind of heavenly feeling. We saw a mass (I guess) where the little choir boys chanted and the organ played.

Saturday night we went to a modern play called *Christophe Colomb* by Paul Claudel. The French put a lot of emphasis on the director who often also takes a role; this one was Jean Louis Barrault (very well-known here). A very strange thing happened at the theater! I sat right next to the French girl who went to Mount Pleasant last year. She recognized me and was so glad to talk with me. Monday she invited me to her house for tea. Her mother, younger sister and some relatives were there. They all talked a mile a minute. I could understand very little except when they spoke directly to me. At any rate, it was enjoyable - their house or apartment, I should say, is really lovely on the inside - big, spacious, many rooms and antiques.

After a while, Marie France (that's her name) took me around her neighborhood. Then we spoke English, thank heavens! She showed me interesting places including the Café Procope. This was the first cafe in Paris. La Fontaine, Voltaire, Rousseau, V. Hugo, Napoleon, and Benjamin Franklin came here! It was quite the intellectual center.

Last night, some of the Fulbrighters gave a surprise birthday party for two kids who had just had birthdays. We had wine and pastry (two of the things we've enjoyed most here!). Also sang - Jay played his guitar - then adjourned to a cafe down the street for more singing and dancing. I can see it now! I'm really going to be all broken up tomorrow when I leave such wonderful friends. I don't think I've ever had so much fun in a group before. Maggie says she will come visit me at Aix.

We've been running around trying to see all the things we haven't visited before. Yesterday I walked up to the Arc de Triomphe and saw the flame burning for the French unknown soldier. Today before class we rushed over to Les Invalides - where Napoleon is buried. His little son, brother, and marshals are also buried there - also General Foch[15]. The building is quite elegant, but Lois and I kept thinking it was such a waste of time, money and energy. Today for lunch we went to the American Embassy. The food so far over here has been quite good, but today I ordered my three most favorite foods - cheeseburger, Coke, and a hot fudge sundae. You can't imagine how good they tasted!

---

15 Ferdinand Foch (1851-1929) served as the Supreme Allied Commander during WWI.

Monsieur Butor gave his lecture today. He is quite well-known and very smart. Six of us will be in the same compartment tomorrow. Sadly, Cathie and another girl will get off at Lyon and then take a train to Grenoble. I sure wish they were coming with me! I still miss you both very much. Please write and say how you like your presents when you get them. Don't forget my new address.

Love,
Barb

Travel Log:

10/19 – 9:15 train from Gare de Lyon. At 2:00 pm, Lois & Cathie got off at Lyon then on to Grenoble. 5:50 pm arrived at Marseille. Took train at 6:30 for Aix, stayed at Hotel de Provence.

10/20 – met Mme Lisle – she gave us a list of addresses. Finally decided on Mme Roman. 360 NF – room has private entrance and looks out on little garden.

October 21

Dear Mother & Daddy –

So I'm writing now that I have a minute. Lois, Cathie, and several of us got on the train Wednesday morning at 9:15. Around 2:00 Lois and Cathie got off at Lyon. They then had to take another train to Grenoble. I was so sad to see Lois go that I almost cried. I certainly do miss her!! The rest of us got off at Marseille around 6:00. We then took another train to Aix. It was quite a long ride.

The Hotel de Provence is very nice. We had a lovely room. Two of the girls went off by themselves and I haven't seen them since; nevertheless I didn't let this bother me. Yesterday Emily, a rather nice girl from Minnesota, and I walked all over town in the rain looking for rooms. Mme Lisle is very nice - she gave us a good list of addresses.

Well, we took a room together at Mme Roman's. Our room looks out on a delightful little garden and we have a private entrance. There seems to be plenty of heat. We also have hot and cold running water in our room. The W.C. is not unpleasant, although it is a far cry from our nice blue tile bathroom at home. We can have two showers a week.

But that's not so bad since we have a sink in the room. It's not at all far from school. We also have breakfast and dinner here.

I was rather astonished at the price - 360 NF a month. This is a little over ½ my check. I don't know if I've done the right thing, but Mme Roman was on the list that Mme Lisle gave us. She seems to be very nice. At least I don't have to worry about finding dinner. She will also give us lunch on Sunday if we let her know ahead of time. The dinner last night was very good and afterwards we all watched TV. The first time I've seen it in France. The TV station is at Marseille so the reception is pretty good.

Besides Emily and me, there is French girl called Françoise. She seems very nice - not at all what you would picture a French girl to be. She is rather timid. There's also a rather good-looking French professor (of geography and history). This morning I read a magazine and played with the dog until the maid brought my breakfast. It is the European type. I had hot chocolate, several pieces of toast, butter and jelly.

There seems to be miles of red tape to register at the school and with the police. I guess we will get it all accomplished eventually. Another very nice Fulbright girl, from Arkansas, lives near us[16]. We are going over to her room tomorrow afternoon to visit.

The people here are much more friendly than in Paris. Last night I was sitting on my suitcase, trying to rest enough to go on. (I was moving from the hotel to Mme Roman's). A man came by on a motor bicycle. He insisted on helping me and wouldn't take a tip. He was from Algeria (not colored).

Many of the streets are very narrow. The buildings are old, but there is much atmosphere. I wish you both could see it too and my room. It is very hard to resist all of the delightful little pastry shops and sometimes I just have to stop.

Well, I must stop and do something about registering. The school for foreigners doesn't start until Nov. 3. Some of the courses really look great. I think the Faculté des Lettres starts next week.

Please write soon - here is my new address:

Chez Mme Roman
10 Rue de la Molle
Aix-en-Provence

Love,
Barb

---

16 Presumably, Dr. Diane Lydia Bronte (1938-2003).

Travel Log:

10/22 – went to Diana's for tea

10/23 – went to Cathedral – lit candle – walked 7 miles in the country

BARBARA IN FRONT OF MME ROMAN'S

BARBARA IN FRONT OF VENDÔME PAVILION

La Fontaine des Quatre-Dauphins[17]

. . . .

17 This is one of the famous fountains in Aix. Émile Zola's father helped build it. Note the narrow streets!

Oct. 24

Dear Mother & Daddy,

Just thought I'd write a short letter telling of my progress. Now I am registered at the School for Foreigners in the Faculté of letters. Today if I have time, I'll go to the police and register with them!

When we registered we had to pay 250 NF. The ride down here was 75 NF. That doesn't leave very much from a check of 642 NF. Of course the Commission will reimburse us, but not until our next check (Dec. 1).

Fortunately I had not used up all my money in Paris. Anyway Emily and I thought the rent here was too high so we started looking around for another place. That night Mme Roman came down to see us, and we explained the problem. After much discussion, I got her to say we could have the room and dinner for 250 NF a month. Before it was 360 NF. I was quite surprised that she would come down so far, but she said she liked us and besides there are 2 of us in one room.

Saturday night the French professor, M. Christian (he teaches high school), Françoise, Emily, a friend of M. Christian, and I all went to the movies. I saw *Jamais le dimanche* again, but this time it was the French version. You can imagine how I enjoyed the cartoons – Porky Pig (in English).

Yesterday I read my Bible and then went to the cathedral with Diana. Another Fulbright. The cathedral was quite impressive, but I didn't get much out of the service. Next week we're going to the Temple (Protestant).

Diana came home with me and Mme Roman invited her to stay for Sunday dinner. Of course she had to pay for it. Then M. Christian, Françoise, Emily and I walked Diana home and then on out into the country. The scenery is really a magnificent sight. We walked around 12 km - I think that's near 7 miles. Saw a French football game, but it's our soccer.

After dinner we watch TV and took turns dancing with M. Christian. Please call Roberta and tell her my news and address. I miss you both so much now that I'd rather write to you! There is approximately 6 hours difference in time so if you think of me at 5 PM, I'll be thinking of you at 11 PM.

Love, Barby

Travel Log:

10/28 – went to Marseille – saw the old port. American Express – Cooke's Tour. Beautiful shops.

10/29 – cooking class. Bought beautiful vase for mother = Louis Phillipe – green mottled

10/30 – [After discussing climbing adventure at Saint-Victoire] – spent the night in the Paul Cézanne Refuge - especially liked Jacques, Eric, and Phillipe.*

10/31 – Met Françoise in Marseille. She and her mother showed us around town. Ate lunch at Cassis celebrated resort. Ocean = blue-green with rocky cliffs coming right down into the water. Later saw Notre Dame de La Garde and climbed to see the Mediterranean (marvelous). Notre Dame protects all the sailors coming into the Vieux Port. Saw Château d'If from distance.

Courses don't start until Nov. 3

Nov. 1

Dear Mother & Daddy –

Thanks so much for the Halloween card. It took me a minute to get the full significance - that I am the witch. Over here, Halloween is known as *Toussaint* (All Saints' Day). The kids get the 31st and the 1st off from school. There is no trick-or-treating - no goblins, witches, etc.

I guess I've been so busy with all my news that I've neglected to answer your questions. I feel sure that I've received all your letters. The birth certificate and diploma came before I left Paris, I think. Your card dated the 26th arrived on 31st, so it must take 4 to 5 days for me to receive your mail.

Mother, I bought your Christmas present the other day, and it should arrive before your vacation. <u>You</u> are not to open it. I would like Daddy to open it and see if it's okay. If it is, he is to wrap it up and hide it. If not, then he must write quickly so I will have time to send something else! Perhaps someone could check the mail if it doesn't arrive before you go.

I've decided that I absolutely must have a 35mm camera. There are so many wonderful [things] that I want to remember - and can also use with teaching. I just can't wait until I get to Switzerland or Germany. I think I can get what I want for around $80. Perhaps you would like to help pay for it as my Christmas gift! If you've decided to send a CARE package, I will be delighted with anything such as food (1), a skirt (3) or sweater (2), stockings, etc. Sometime it would be appreciated if you could send a <u>plate</u>. Mme Roman collects plates and she might like one from the US. Also 2 maps of the US - one for me and another for one of the borders who teaches geography.

I had a fabulous weekend. Saturday, I went to the cooking class and learned how to make *bouillabaisse* - a very famous fish soup here in Provence. The teacher is a delightful little man. We pay 4 NF (around 80¢). We eat what we make. This *bouillabaisse* took 7 different kinds of fish. You should've seen my face when I was cleaning one of them. Also we saved some of the heads and tails and boiled them in another pot!!!

We also made tomatoes provençales and a delicious fruit salad. You put bananas, pears, orange sections, pineapples, all of which have been sliced, and cherries together. Then add sugar, white wine, and rum. It's most delicious.

Sunday 3 of us joined the excursionists and rode over to the rocky mountain called Saint Victoire. Cézanne made it very famous with his painting. We parked a good ways away, and I was practically dead when we reached the refuge, which is actually at the foot of the mountain. There were several demonstrations of mountain climbing and descending with a wounded person. They weren't very friendly at first and we had contemplated going home early; however, after the lunch and <u>wine</u>, everyone became more cordial.

You'll never guess what happened next! They insisted that we climb the mountain with them. Well we didn't want to lose their friendship so off we went! They tied a rope around each person's waist. The boy ahead of me was extremely good and the man behind me told me where to put my feet and hands. I started up and wanted to go back down, but there was no place to go. They knew some English and kept shouting encouraging English phrases, but most of the time we spoke French. I kept asking where do I put my right foot, then my left, etc. They seemed to enjoy us and insisted that we come back to spend the night.

There were girls there too!! Most of these French kids are really terrific if you get to know them.[18]

Today (Oct. 31) Emily and I met Françoise (she boards here) in Marseille and she and her mother drove us all around town showing us the sites. They took us to lunch at Cassis near Marseille. The water was a beautiful blue-green and the rocky hills came right down into the water. At Marseille we mounted a very high church and looked out over the whole town. I saw Château d'If from a distance. Dumas made this very famous in his book, *The Count of Monte Cristo*. Marseille is quite lovely even though it doesn't have the same beauty as Paris.

I've collected 2 stones for you, Daddy. One from Saint Victoire and another from the shores of the Mediterranean!! I'm beginning to think of Christmas vacation. Would like very much to visit the Côte d'Azur and Italy. I sure wish you were here with me.

Love, Barb

---

18 Barbara reminisced about this trip when attending a "Cézanne in Provence" exhibit at the National Gallery of Art in Washington, DC in 2006.

Barbara's Photo of Montagne Sainte-Victoire

Thanks so much for the <u>news</u>

Nov. 4

Dear Mother & Daddy,

You can't imagine how delighted I was to get your box of cookies and candy! It was very thoughtful of you, and I certainly do appreciate it. I gave one of the little Halloween bags to my roommate. She was delighted and hopes that her mother will send cookies for Christmas.

Today I attended the general meeting for all the foreign students at the Institut. Later there was a reception with champagne and cookies. The Admiral of the US 6th fleet was there. It seems they are in Marseille now.

You asked if the Main Street in Aix is really that picturesque. Yes, it certainly is! There are tall sycamore trees along the sides and many lovely fountains. I really enjoy the other streets more because they are so narrow. There are many, many little stores and shops. There is only one store in town where you can buy a lot of goods at once. Usually you have to go to a different store for each article.

Eggs, cheese, and milk are at the *crèmerie*; bread and rolls at a *boulangerie*; little cakes and bonbons at a *patisserie*; meat at a *bouchère*, etc.

You asked about my Christmas list. I believe it is in my last letter. My main desire is to buy a camera. I've been looking around. I like Royer Savoy very much. It seems you need a light meter for a 35mm camera so I would rather have it included in the camera. The Retinette by Kodak looks nice, but I don't think I need to spend over $80. Daddy, I wonder if you could go to a camera store in Wilmington and find out a few things for me:

1. Is the Royer Savoy sold in the US? And can you get it repaired easily? (There is a 3 yr guarantee)
2. Which is the better camera and also the more expensive? I can get the Royer Savor for 395 NF or about $80.

Many people say, of course, I should wait until I get to Germany or Switzerland; however, the way things look now, it will be a long time before I make it, if ever, and I want the camera now!

Oh yes! Another nightshirt would do fine, although it's warmer here than in Paris. Please send the pictures with your box. I'm sorry the ones of the gardens weren't very good. Perhaps if I have a light meter on the new camera, I will do better. I could use some stockings since I have to wear them all the time. The kids over here wear stockings and heels to class. I don't see how they stand it.

Tomorrow I start my courses. Some of them look very interesting. Many are about contemporary literature and that is my weakest point. I know hardly anything at all. I just finished reading *La Peste*[19] by Albert Camus so at least I have read one contemporary novel.

I've got to hurry up and buy some little Christmas presents for Gladys, Roberta, Kathy, and Margie - also Christmas cards, which are not out yet. If they don't get things on time, perhaps you can explain for me. (Could you me send Jerry's address?). I sort of hope Gladys won't come for Christmas because I want to go to Italy, but of course, I can't tell her that. If you were coming, perhaps she would wait, but Spring is a long way off; however, if you just saw Paris and Aix your trip would be worth it.

I know you must be looking forward to the hunting season, Daddy. Good luck and tell everyone I said "hello".

I wrote a letter to Miss Stewart and received an answer. She is very sweet. Also I've heard some from Al.

Love, Barb

....

19 *The Plague.*

Nov. 8 (Election Night)

Dear Mother & Daddy –

Tonight I'm anxiously waiting to hear the results of the election. It is 10:30 here, but only 4:30 in the US. I found a store that sells 2 New York papers so I should find out sometime tomorrow. Do write me all the details!! Kennedy & Nixon have been shown on the TV here almost every night.

I'm sorry if this letter is a bit late. I intended to write last night, but all of a sudden I had a date, and you know me - I couldn't pass it up. His name is Georges and he's from Nice. His mother is French; father, Italian. We saw a Russian movie with French dialogue! Georges is tall and dark - not quite as handsome as he thinks he is.

Gladys wrote saying that she won't be able to come. I'm sorry I won't be able to see her, but it's sort of a relief. Now I can plan something for Christmas. Emily and I made a tentative schedule where we will spend Christmas in Nice, 3 days in Florence, 4 days in Rome, etc. I just can't believe that we might actually get to see some of these places.

I tried to get my ointment prescription fulfilled last week! What a struggle! Two of the stores couldn't tell what the last ingredient was. Also they didn't understand the measurements. The third pharmacy was very nice. They said they would try to fix something up. The result looks and smells very much like the ointment so I think it will do.

I asked Mme Lisle the name of a doctor so I can get a flu shot. She thought I was crazy and said not to worry. Frankly, I doubt that there is such thing over here. Maybe when I go to Marseille next, I can ask the American consulate.

Last Saturday Diana and I went to Marseille. We got on one of the little sightseeing boats for the Château d'If. It was a lovely day, but the sea was very bad. It became too rough so the captain brought us back to port and took us on a tour of all the big ships at the port. We met a very nice French soldier who had been on leave and was going back to Algeria. Afterwards we had a cup of coffee together and exchanged addresses. Today Diana and I received a postcard from him in Algeria!

One afternoon Françoise's parents came over & took us (Emily and me) to tea. They are lovely people! I found out today that the mother of the young man boarding with us here at Mme Roman's had a stroke so he had to go home. It's a shame.

Also he was thinking of inviting us to Corsica. I won't need 2 maps of the US now although I could still use one if you send it.

Sunday I went to the Protestant church here. It was most delightful! The minister is very well known in Europe. Many of the American and English students go there. It was communion. We stood together in front of the church and took the bread and wine together. I'm starting to memorize the Lord's Prayer in French. Instead of saying "forever and ever," they say *"aux siècles des siècles"* (from centuries to centuries).

Then I went out to Diana's - she has a little stove in her room. We had ravioli, bread, cheese, fruit, tomatoes, coffee, and patisserie.

Went back to the church at 5:00 because the minister was showing slides of US. They're very much astonished that a country as huge as we have, have only 1 law / 1 coinage / 1 language, etc. Also the importance of the car and the highways. Also our churches - the American churches are not necessarily the richest, but they are always the most generous!

I think a plate from Delaware would be nice for Mme Roman. I would love to have one of "Old College."[20] Yesterday, I bought Daddy's Christmas

---

20 Old College: a building at the University of Delaware

present so Mother, you can open <u>his</u> & wrap it up for me in colored paper.

Most of the courses seem quite interesting. I just hope I don't have to work too hard. It's a bit of a strain living in a foreign country.

You pronounce *Rue de la Molle* as though Molle rhymed with hull (of a ship).

Do let me know when you get the presents and also their condition. I was so glad to hear that you think I should get a camera now.

Write soon I miss you both-

Love,
Barbie

PS - When you get to Virginia, tell everyone "hello" for me.

Joyeux Noël

Dear Mother & Dad,

Here is a sample of the Xmas cards I bought!. Cute, but inexpensive.

Not much news - You can imagine how delighted I was with the Election!! Did Mr. Pollari make it - also what about Boggs, Fiear, Corvel, etc.?

I'm going to another cooking class Sat. I may go somewhere over the week-end Nov. 11 is a holiday here!

I found out that it costs $12.00 in 3 minutes to call home. If you get real lonely maybe I could call collect sometime although $12.00 is quite a lot! I will try to get an Xmas present for Sue-Ellen. Love, Barb

Nov. 10

Dear Mother & Dad,

Here is a sample of the Christmas cards I bought! Cute, but inexpensive.

Not much news. You can imagine how delighted I was with the election! Did Mr. Pollari make it - also what about Boggs, Frear, Corvel, etc.?

I'm going to another cooking class Sat. I may go somewhere over the weekend. Nov. 11 is a holiday here!

I found out that it cost $12.00 for 3 minutes to call home. If you get real lonely maybe I could call collect sometime, although $12.00 is quite a lot! I will try to get a Christmas present for Sue-Ellen.

Love, Barb

Travel Log:

11/12 – Cooking class – *Boeuf en Daube, Haricots vertes, Tartes*. After cooking class took autocar for Fréjus delightful countryside (saw lots of vineyards). At Fréjus, took a bus to St. Raphael and met Emily and Jean Kinnon[21] – walked around – went into Byzantine-style church – then took bus to Cannes.

11/13 – walked along sea – La Croisette famous street in Cannes. Water and mountains are out of this world. Saw Carlton Hotel – all white with fancy balconies and 2 black domes. Walked around and met 2 American medical students from Rome. Jean and I went back to hotel. Emily on to Grasse.

---

21 Presumably Jean McLennan Kinnon (1935-2009).

La Côte d'Azur
CANNES (A.-M.)
2099 - La Croisette et le Suquet, au premier plan la terrasse du Martinez.

Dear Mother & Dad,
  Here I am in Cannes. It is one of the most beautiful places I have ever seen. It is prettier than Miami because you have a combination of mts. and water.
  Carolyn, a girl from Liverpool, England, & I decided to take a little tour. We packed some food & are wearing the same clothes. Yesterday I met them in St. Raphael also on the Côte d'Azur. This is not the peak season. The Carlton & other large Hotels are opening around Dec. 15. We will go on to Colour & Genoa before returning to Paris. Wish you were here! Love, Barb

PAR AVION

Mr & Mrs W. R. [—]
504 Springhill Ave.
Wilmington 3, Delaware
U.S.A.

PAR AVION

Please keep this card!!

11/13

Dear Mother & Dad,

Here I am in Cannes. It is one of the most beautiful places I have ever seen! It is prettier than Miami because you have a combination of mts. and water!

Emily, a girl from Liverpool, England, and I decided to take a little tour. We packed some food & are wearing the same clothes. Yesterday I met them in St. Raphael - also on the Cote d'Azur. This is not the peak season. The Carlton and other large hotels are opening around Dec. 19. We may go on to Grasse before returning to Aix. Wish you were here!!

Love, Barb

Don't worry about the flash attachment for now.

11/14

Dear Dad,

Please get the camera as <u>soon</u> as you can! I hate to spend a lot of money for something I don't know much about! Will there be any trouble with customs? I spent another night in Cannes and came home this morning. I have never seen such beautiful countryside. Received a letter from Aunt Ruby. Best of luck on your hunting expedition.

Love, Barb

November 14

Dear Mother & Daddy –

I suppose I should really get busy with my studying, but everything seems a little vague. I should hand in a paper on the humanism of Rabelais [on] Friday so I guess that will keep me busy. I want to tell you about my recent activities anyway!!

Thursday night the head of our cooking class, a delightful old man with white hair, took me to dinner and what a dinner!! Evidently the *Restaurant Vendôme* is celebrating the hunting season and each Thursday night, they have a big gala dinner. There was an orchestra and the doormen were dressed up as hunters - redcoats, white pants, caps, etc. In one corner there was a stand attractively arranged with all sorts of dead wild birds!

Well, to begin, we had *La Crème Reine Margot* (I'm reading from my souvenir menu). This is a creamed chicken soup with tiny bits of chicken and toast. A white wine was served.

Then we had *Le Cuissot de daim Bavaroise* - or in other words, some kind of deer meat. It was absolutely delicious - no greasy taste at all - also a good gravy and applesauce (warm). A red wine was served.

Next we had *La Bécasses Sautée au champagne* - some kind of little bird - another red wine was served. Also with this, a salad of lettuce, endive, and chopped almonds. Then we had water to wash out the wine taste and a large selection of cheese from which to pick. I chose gruyére which is very close to what we call Swiss cheese.

For dessert we had *La Poire Belle Hélène*. This is a pear (sort of steamed, at least it wasn't raw) sitting in a dish of ice-cream over which chocolate sauce is poured. It is accompanied with little cookies and champagne. Finally a demitasse of coffee was served. During and after dinner, there were a few games - I won a little bottle of perfume. Dinner started at 9:15; we left at midnight. The dancing had just started but my partner was a little old so we didn't indulge. I wore my black wool dress, red shoes and good coat.

The dinner cost 35 NF which may not seem like too much if you think of $7.00 but it's really a lot of money over here on my standards. When you are eating your turkey dinner, don't feel too sorry for me although I would still prefer the turkey and dressing. I'm afraid I'll never become a Frenchman because I like my own life too much!! Do tell anyone that might be interested about my dinner - Aunt Ruby, grandmother, etc.

The cooking class was delightful too on Saturday. We cut up chunks of beef with bay leaves, orange rind, onions stuck with cloves and a bottle of red wine. In a pressure cooker, it was finished in about 2 ½ hours. You'll be interested in the different stoves. The class is held in the homemaking house for girls in Aix, and they must learn to use all kinds. There are 4 stoves - one burns coal; one, bottled gas; another has gas somewhat like ours; the last is electric.

After the cooking class, I took a bus to Fréjus. Then I changed and took another bus a short distance to St. Raphael. Here I met Emily and a lovely girl from Liverpool, England. We walked around admiring the Mediterranean Sea, palm trees, and houses. After about two hours, we took the bus to Cannes.

Cannes is really one of the most beautiful places in the world. It is on one of the bays of the Mediterranean with high mountains in the distance. We found a very nice hotel back from the water (less costly and most of those along the water were closed). Our room had a balcony overlooking the city and water. We paid about 6 NF each night. Sunday we walked along the main street by the sea. They also have palm trees and beautiful hotels. It reminds you a little of Miami. Emily was busy taking pictures and we lost her. When we found her again, she wasn't upset so we left her again. I had originally planned to go onto Grasse, but Jean and I decided to stay and go back to the same room at the hotel. We really explored the city.

At dinner time, we went into a self-service restaurant - got a very good meal for 5 NF and met two American medical students from Rome. They were on their way to Paris so I told them some of the high spots to see! What delightful plain, common, American names they have - Bill Martin and Jack Fisher.

This morning Jean and I took the train back to Marseille and then a bus back to Aix - we got back in time for our class (only 1 on Monday).

Tomorrow I'm going to buy some cologne water for Roberta, Glady, Cathie, Margie, Sue-Ellen, and Aunt Ruby. The store will send it. It looks attractive and it's not too expensive. I will need to cash a traveler's check and use the rest of the money to live on until the arrival of the December check.

Very best wishes for your vacation. I will be thinking of you and I will send some letters to grandmother. Tell everyone "hello." Daddy - thanks so much for seeing about the camera for me.

Love, Barb

[Letter sent to Barbara's grandmother's address in Bridgewater, Virginia]

Nov. 18

Dear Mother & Daddy –

Well, by the time you read this you will be on vacation. I hope you're having lots of fun - eating, hunting, buying antiques, etc.!

There's not much news. I got back the last pictures I took today. Some of them are quite good- the Cathedral at Chartres, the Arc de Triomphe, a lady dressed in a costume selling lace hats, etc.

I was very unhappy to read in the paper I bought this morning that Clark Gable had died. The *New*

York Herald Tribune puts out a European edition which gets on the stands very early. I can also get the *New York Times* in the evening.

Last night I went to the Franco-Anglo Club. It was very exciting. The French kids are delightful and are particularly interested in us because they are studying English (the ones in the club). The French kids learn English with a British accent. Some of them have trouble understanding Americans unless we speak slowly. We elected officers for the club, and afterward there was dancing. The sponsors of the club are a lovely couple. He is American and she is French.

A committee of former Fulbrights from Marseille is coming over to Aix Sunday to show us around the town and to take us out to lunch. That seems very hospitable to me.

I'm going to the cooking class again Saturday. We are making some kind of dish with rabbit. Saturday night Diana and I are supposed to go out on a double date was Georges and a friend of his from Marseille. Some of these boys are rather unpredictable!

I told you about the nice group of students we met the Sunday we went out to Saint Victoire. Last night one of the boys called me up and asked me to a party Saturday night. You might know I would have made other plans! Anyway, he is coming over to see me for a few minutes tonight. You should see me speaking French over the telephone! It's much harder when you can't see a face.

The weather in Aix is a little warmer than in Wilmington. It's almost time for me to put the lining in my coat. The room is comfortable although I'd like to get rid of my roommate! The heat went off [for] a few days, but it has been fixed and it's working fine. I wish I could get a single room, but I don't want to leave my friends here, so perhaps I will just ignore Emily. I'm looking forward to receiving my Christmas package.

Love,
Barb

Read this to Aunt Ruby, too.

Nov. 23

Hope you are having fun and behaving yourselves! Also, Daddy, you must not go over your limit of turkeys, deer, bears, etc. Ha! Ha!

I had a lovely weekend. Saturday night Diana and I went with Georges and his friends to a ball. It began at 10:00 and continued until dawn; however, we didn't stay to the end, thank goodness. I got home at 4:30. The dance was very nice. The French kids do all sorts of dances - there is much more variety. The boys are rather independent. One time Georges danced with one of the other girls, which was quite alright; however, I went into another room and danced with one of the English boys at the Institute. Georges came after me and was not too happy! I hope I'm not going to go around on this temperamental merry-go-round again!

Sunday many of the former French Fulbrights to the US came to Aix and took us on a tour. The head of our tour was a M. Coste. He's one of my teachers and has written a book about Aix and Provence which we use for a textbook. Then we had a delicious dinner and another tour. You might know I would sit next to M. Ruff! It was enjoyable, but we spoke French the entire time. He recalls Mr. Neel and says that he was a little "flighty". He had trouble passing his exams. M. Ruff says Mrs. Neel was much more intelligent and reasonable. It sounds as though M. Ruff sure had his number! I thought you would have been in complete agreement.

Friday night Emily and I went to a sort of student nightclub here in Aix. It's called the *Hot Club*. You crawl into a little red door in the side of the wall and then go down some rather steep stairs. At the bottom, everything looks like a cave. People are drinking and dancing. The night we went, most of the kids there were from the American Institute. They are over here for their junior year abroad. There are at least 50 of them. Most of them are nice kids, but they seemed a good deal younger than us. Some of them are having quite a difficult time with their French. Heaven knows I have my problems, but I'm certainly thankful I finished college. The last two years are very important!

The boys who invited us to go to the party Saturday night (I couldn't go) met Emily, Diana, and me in Marseille today. We took a boat out to the

Château d'If. The water in the port was quite calm, but when we got out to sea, it was really rough - water was spraying all over us so we had to come back. This is the second time this happened to me!! I wonder if I'll ever make it?[22]

Yesterday I heard the Voice of America on the radio. It was being broadcast from Washington-the transmitter is in Munich, Germany.

Did I tell you, Jackie Kennedy studied here in Aix for a few months? She has relatives near Avignon. All her relatives sent congratulations after the election.

I've been trying to decide what to do next year. As if I didn't have enough problems already. I would like to go to college again, but it's so hard to go through all the red tape in applying that I think I'll wait a year. Perhaps next January or February, you could call the placement bureau at the University of Delaware and ask them to send me their bulletins for job applications teaching, that is. There will be a cost, but I doubt that it will be too much.

Tomorrow some of us are going out to dinner to celebrate Thanksgiving. There won't be a turkey,

---

22 Barbara told that she was wearing a white blouse and, due to it getting quite wet, she had to borrow a cover-up from one of her friends.

but I'm planning on steak and wine, so that's a good second choice.

When you get home, could you send me Eleanor's and Mr. Neel's address? I should send them Christmas cards.

I received a letter in the mail from Air France today saying they have a package for me; however, the customs people are charging me 160 NF!! I will have to cash 2 travelers checks and I already cashed 2. I just feel like sending it back and having you send me the money; however, that would cause you a lot of trouble and I guess they would still get me when I took the camera back home. I hope the gifts I sent you won't be too expensive! We will have to stop sending gifts. I can't afford the duty!

Diana's parents are giving her a Volkswagen for Christmas and she also has two boy friends from England coming down (they are Americans). I can't decide whether to spend Christmas with them or to go with Lois and Cathie. The car would be cheaper! Sure wish you both could be here!!

Love, Barb

Nov. 27
(Sunday)

Dear Mother & Daddy –

    I have just come back from church. It was very nice. I'm sorry I don't go every Sunday but there always seems to be something going on, especially on weekends! They had four candles upfront - only one was lighted. They will light a new one with each Sunday before Christmas. I shared a book with the man next to me, and after the service found out that he was from Canada. The people from Canada are much more like us than those from England.

    I've been having a time trying to remember to use the "tu" form in French. We say "you" always for the second person; however, the French say tu to those people whom they know well; it is especially popular with the students. I never paid much attention to it because I never thought I would know anyone that well! Over here, I have to use it most of the time, or my friends will think I'm not friendly.

    My Thanksgiving dinner was quite nice. Some of us went to a darling little restaurant called *La*

Tartane. I had a plate of assorted meats as the hors d'oeuvre. Then some ravioli, then a steak served on lettuce, ice cream, bread, and wine (rosé). The owner has an interest in Americans because his father runs a restaurant in New York. He brought out a bottle of champagne for us. There was a little old man there who spoke with us. I found out that he has made movies with Simone Signoret, Louis Jordan, Maurice Chevalier, etc. There were wine bottles hanging all over the ceiling for atmosphere. I said I would like to buy one, so the man gave each one of us a bottle.

I wonder if you could send me the addresses of George and Mary Lou, Aunt Esther, and Uncle Massey?[23] I have sent most of my Christmas cards now.

After church, I ate dinner at Mme Roman's since I had missed my dinner Thursday night. We also asked Diana and Jackson over so it was a gay little group. Mme Roman wasn't there! She was very happy to get the 10 NF from our friends for the meal though! After lunch, we walked down to the *Cours Mirabeau* and met some of our friends at a café. Some of them were French.

....

23 [Cousin] Mary Lou Riddleberger Barnes (1930-2015); Esther Heltzel Miller (1900-1990); and Rev. Massey Mott Heltzel (1915-1980)

Georges wrote a letter for me to the customs officials, saying that I did not intend to sell the camera; it is strictly personal. I hope they will lower the tax, but if not, I will have to pay it.

Yesterday the Faculty of Letters had a reception for foreign students. We enjoyed it although there was no champagne. We were given a tour of the new boys' dorms, which are very lovely. There is a sink and a big picture window with balcony in each room - also bed, desk, closet, bookshelves. Only one boy to a room! They have a beautiful view of the mountains and Saint Victoire. Also a lovely courtyard with the fountain. You can't beat that at the University of Delaware! The cost is 55 NF a month ($11.00).

The cooking class is still a big success. The last time we prepared rabbit and little pastries which are a cross between donuts and creampuffs. You drop the batter into cooking oil. The little balls swell up and turned themselves over when they are brown. If you want, you can fill them like cream puffs. This time we made a fish dish with cod, stuffed tomatoes, and *Pêche Melba*.

I am anxiously awaiting the arrival of my check which should come this week. I have to buy Al a present and get some shoes out of the repair shop. I can't imagine what it will be like to hold nine $100 NF bills in my hand at once! We should be paid the regular 642 NF and 75 NF for travel and 250 NF for tuition.

The other night I went with Georges to a movie of Gérard Philipe's. He is dead now - died at an early age – [and] was a matinee idol of France. I saw him in New York two years ago. The film was good, *La Chartreuse de Parme*, but he was excellent.

I received a lovely letter from Glady and also a cute card on Thanksgiving day.

Hope you're having success, Daddy. I tell all of my friends that my father is out hunting deer and turkey. Many of the kids were surprised to learn that there is still such a thing as wild turkeys! They thought they were all domesticated these days. I have a good idea whose <u>car</u> you took for the hunting expedition. If it's mine, just make sure that all the blood is washed off.

Last night I got a radio station from Luxembourg which played good old American and English records. It almost gave me a queer feeling to hear "Here Comes Santa Claus" in English.

Love, Barb

Cours Mirabeau

Dec. 4 (Sunday)

Dear Mother and Daddy,

Received a letter and postcard from you yesterday. I'm glad to hear of your activities! Mother, you never said what you thought of the picture, *Ben Hur*. It was rather long, wasn't it – with Charlton Heston?

I have some very good news about the camera! First, I received an answer to my letter, saying I would have to pay 160 NF, but would be reimbursed when I left France if I come in person to the customs office and signed a form. Saturday, Emily and I went out to the airport, which is quite beautiful! Much larger and prettier than New Castle. I explained again that I was not going to sell the camera – I was a student! They were just lovely to us and let us have the packages for only a small storage charge, about $2. They were probably violating a law since they didn't charge me anything. Emily has heard that if you declare a package under $10, there is no problem.

At any rate, I am just thrilled with the camera! It's just what I wanted! Not too difficult to operate. I'm going to buy some film with only 20 shots on it and practice around here in Aix before I go on vacation. There is another small problem, but I'm not going to worry too much – I completely forgot to tell you to get a case for the camera. It's very bad for the camera to carry it around without the case for protection. I asked in several stores for a case, but this model Kodak is not sold in France yet, so I can't find one. None of the other cases will fit! I think I'll just wrap it up in my raincoat envelope when I carry it around. Everyone in the camera stores seems to be quite fascinated with it. It must be the latest thing! If you should decide to send me a case, make sure you value it under $10, <u>please</u>.

Things have been very busy this week. I finally met Mme Olagnon, the lady Dr. St. Aubyn[24] knows. She invited me back to tea Thursday and to meet her daughter. Her daughter and another girl were there. We had a very good time. I ended up by joining a club – or musical group which allows to me to attend some very fine concerts. Friday night I went with the friend to a concert on ballet. It was very interesting, but I just can't get too thrilled over ballet! Mme Olagnon's husband has died, I think. Anyway, now she is called Mme Arnaud. Dr. St. Aubyn will be surprised!

---

24 Dr. Frederic Chase St. Aubyn (1921-2004), a French professor at the University of Delaware and Barbara's faculty advisor.

Monday night I went to a play, *L'Avare* by Moliere – enjoyed it a great deal since I am a great fan of Moliere's.

The Franco-Anglo club was fun also this week on Wednesday night. It was American night, so we spoke English and sang American cowboy songs. They got quite a bang out of singing "Jimmy Crack Corn" (*the blue-tail fly*). I met some lovely girls who are studying English and American lit. They wanted to meet with me to speak French and <u>English</u>. I went to see one of them Friday afternoon. The other one came over; and we had a delightful time comparing countries, customs, languages, etc. They helped me some with my phonetics course. In literature, they are studying Washington Irving, Hawthorne, Robert Frost, and Frank Norris. Maybe I can help them since I've studied all these people!

I had another interesting experience with the cooking course Saturday morning. It was my turn to meet M. Giniès, the teacher, and go to the market with him. He needs someone to help him carry the food. First, we went to the outdoor markets, which cover several blocks and sell everything from chestnuts to shoes and heaters! We bought chestnuts and spinach. You know, I think that was the first time I really understood what raw spinach looks like! Then we went to a little shop where they sell only fish and bought crabs – then to a butcher's for lamb chops – then to a *crèmerie* for butter and eggs. All the time I carried a packsack on my back. What a sight, eh!

Last night I saw a good movie with Diana and Jean. Georges went home for the weekend to Nice. How would you like to live in Nice! Today, Jean, Emily, Manuel (Fr. girl here at Mme Roman's) and I took a walk. We visited Cezanne's workshop then walked in the country and picked wildflowers. On the way, I saw some men leading three horses into the butcher's store. I felt so sorry for them. I'm sure they knew what was going to happen. They were almost screaming. I have a feeling I may have eaten some horse meat at the Cité; my only hope is since horse meat is expensive in France, maybe the Cité can't afford it.

I bought myself a beautiful sky blue mohair sweater. I didn't really need it since I have some Christmas presents coming, but it is quite lovely.

Perhaps I will go to Spain with Emily after all! We seem to be getting along well now, and it's nice to know with whom you're traveling. I would love to see Madrid and the Rock of Gibraltar. Italy would probably be nicer in the spring and maybe there is a slight chance that you can go with me. What do you think? I think it would be nice to call home on Christmas Day between 9:00 – 12:00 your time. Does that suit you?

Love,
Barb

Dec. 11 (Sunday)

Dear Mother & Daddy –

Glad to hear you got home safely and had a good time! If my package to Aunt Ruby has arrived, then the one to Sue-Ellen and the other girls must have arrived too. If you want to open your packages before Christmas go ahead. I've arranged for another little surprise, and I'm sure it can't break! I also plan to call home Christmas day, if it's agreeable to you. Don't worry though if I can't get through because I plan to be in Madrid and heaven only knows what the Spanish phones are like!

I haven't received any mail for 3 days. I don't know if it just happened or if it's due to an airplane strike! Also there's a TV strike here. Politics are getting quite hot too! I hear there's been some fighting in Paris about the Algerian problem. December 13 is the day for de Gaulle's referendum.[25] If he isn't supported, I don't know what will happen to the government, probably another change! It reminds me of our problem in the Civil War. It is only right to give Algeria complete independence, but the Arabs are so ruthless…!

....

25 Apparently a referendum on Algerian self-determination.

Also France needs the Algerian economy. A lot of Frenchman are living in Algeria now.

I was very happy to receive the picture of Grandmother. I think it's quite good!

Emily and I found out that Mme Roman is willing to rent some of her rooms without pension so we demanded the same treatment. She has been so frantic trying to find boarders that she agreed. We will get the room for 90 NF ($18) each starting in January. Of course we will miss the dinners, but the food at the Cité is very good and costs only 1 NF per meal.

All my shoes have been run down due to much walking and the hard streets. I've now gotten 3 pairs fixed. The shoe repair man is delightful. His shop is nothing to look at, but he does a good job. I got him to put little metal pieces on the heels of my loafers to keep them from wearing down so soon.

I bought a little charm for my bracelet. It is a darling little palette which painters use. It reminds me of Cézanne, which reminds me of Saint Victoire. I also may get a little fleur-de-lis that I saw in Marseille.

One of my girlfriends from Paris is planning to visit me a few days this week. She almost has finished her <u>Doctor's Degree</u> in comparative literature at University of North Carolina. Needless to say, she makes me feel quite stupid. She will meet some other people who are coming to Aix and then go on to Italy.

Emily and I hope to leave next Sunday or Monday for Spain. I think the weather will be much better there than Italy just now. It has really been cold here in Aix the last few days!

The people of Aix have invited all the foreign students to a *Fête de Nöel* – kind of reception in the afternoon. Each country will sing its own Christmas carols.

Thursday night the Franco-Anglo club is having a Christmas dinner. It should be quite a lot of fun. Most of my French friends are coming - also English and American friends.

Diana is getting her car, a brand-new Simca[26], either today or tomorrow. It is a lovely present, but I'd hate to have to worry about getting it back home with me.

I received a list of sailing dates from the Fulbright commission today. July 20 or July 27 seem like good dates, but they neglected to give the names of the ships. I would like very much to see England and to sail from Southampton. After Christmas I must find out about sending my trunk home ahead of time. I would love to get rid of it sometime in June. Do you think it could

---

26 A French automobile.

go through customs without me and maybe you could pick it up in New York?

Today Georges, another friend, and I went to visit one of our French friends who was in a serious automobile accident. He had a fractured skull and was in a coma for 4 or 5 hours. We just missed him at the hospital so we went to his home in Avignon. He's much better now, but doesn't plan to return to school until January. His car was completely demolished! Georges asked him what kind of car he was going to buy now and his mother said, "Nothing." Mothers seem to have exactly the same sentiment whether they live in France or America! My French friends have been a big help with my comprehension. Sometimes they brag about me, which makes me embarrassed because I really don't know as much as they think!

Today I also went to cooking class. We made chicken with a delightful sauce (it had white wine in it). Also apple pie (not very different from ours!).

I've been studying the pamphlet about my camera. I think I understand it all. Emily watched me while I put the film in it.

Write soon

Love, Barb

PS – Don't forget to include me in your gift to Margie. I bought her a lovely card the other day!

BARBARA'S CHARM BRACELET

L-R: camel (Morocco); wine (Italy); roulette wheel (Monaco); bagpipe (Scotland); ocean liner; son (Warren), ski chalet (Switzerland); daughter (Kim); bull (Spain); Eiffel Tower (France); Gryphon (?); Big Ben (England); palette; Arc de Triomphe (France).

Dec. 16

Friday

Dear Mother & Daddy –

This has really been one busy week! I've hardly had time to breathe. I feel as if though Christmas has already come. I received a beautiful yellow-print, roll-up sleeve blouse from Roberta. She also sent me a charm (a darling little Christmas tree) so I even have a tree now. I hope you do too! I'm afraid I should send her something more, but I'll bring her a present when I come.

[Aunt] Waltine and Denis[27] sent me a pair of pajamas and a nice long letter. Grandmother sent me two pair of pants. I really didn't expect to get anything from them this year. Mme Roman's plate also arrived. She is thrilled with it - even kissed me for it, Ha! Ha! I was glad to see the pictures I took. The other roll turned out better, but that was because of the weather. Also was thrilled with the magazine about Kennedy. I really have a lot of faith in him. I think he is just what our country needs! I was also delighted to see that University

----

27 Naomi Waltine Snow Hoover (1916-1963) and Harry Denis Hoover (1913-2005).

of Delaware made the cover of the Mortarboard Quarterly. Did you see the picture of us inside?

Sure hope your presents arrived okay. As I said before, I've also planned another little surprise. I still plan to call Christmas if I can get through - sometime in the morning your time. My last package from you has not arrived as of yet, but I really feel as though I've already had enough.

Today I bought some *santons*[28]. They are little painted, baked clay figures very popular in Provence. You can put them with the crèche at Christmas time. They are just lovely. I bought a little old man with a beard and his wife is wearing a shawl. Also bought a young girl in a provençale dress. She is carrying a water pitcher.

....
28 Little saints. These figures were a treasured possession of Barbara's.

Cricket came down from Paris Tuesday night. She didn't leave until this morning. I enjoyed seeing her very much. She almost has her doctor's degree from the University of North Carolina. She wants me to apply for a job at 2 private schools in Richmond - St. Catherine's and Collegiate; however, the money wouldn't be as good as I could get in Delaware or California.

She is going to Italy with 3 American boys. We put them up last night at Mme Roman's. She really seems to enjoy herself, I think. I'm so glad I'm in Aix. It rained in Paris for 18 days straight! Also, she has no contact with French students. She likes my friends very much. One afternoon we went to one of the girl's rooms and played games (don't worry it was quite respectable). Another afternoon we went to Avignon again to see our friend Joël, who was in an accident. He is recovering from a fractured skull. Unfortunately, his head hurts him still quite a bit and he's tired of being sick.

The people of Aix gave all the foreign students a party, a *Fête de Nöel*. The Germans, English, and Americans sang their respective Christmas carols. Naturally, I thought the American ones were by far the best. I get the impression sometime that Europeans think we are crude and money-minded, but they often can't keep from liking us in spite of themselves. Very few American students are snobbish. We had white wine - the closest one to champagne, assorted sandwiches, and cookies.

Last night I went to the Christmas dinner at the Franco-Anglo club. The food was nothing to brag about, but we had a marvelous time. Afterward we sang and danced. Georges went to Avignon and then to the dinner also. Cricket thinks he's very nice. I suppose it would be quite impossible for us to ever get together, but he certainly has all the other boys I've known beat [by] a block. I guess I've just never known the right one.

Emily and I are very excited today. We are packing to go to Spain. We will take the midnight train out of Marseille for Barcelona. It takes 11 hours to get there. The only other train leaves at noon, and we would rather not arrive in Barcelona at 11:00 at night. If you would like to write one, send the letters to American Express, Barcelona. We also plan to come back through there. Don't write to the Fulbright Commission asking for us, because we are going two days before vacation. Practically everyone is leaving early, but I'd just as soon the Commission didn't find out.

After Barcelona, we want to go on to Madrid and then south. I was really furious the other day. We tried to get some of our francs converted into pesetas and the bank wouldn't do it because we were foreigners. They will convert dollars or pesetas into francs, but not the other way around. We will have to find a bank in Barcelona to change our money!

    I will send you cards from time to time. I hope to be talking to you before too long. Merry Christmas. You must do everything just as though I were there and do write me a long description of Margie's wedding.

Love, Barb

12/17

Took 12:30 AM train out of Marseille. Soldiers shared compartment – little sleep. Arrived at Portbou at 8:00, went through customs, then took train to Barcelona and arrived at 1 PM.

Boy sharing compartment helped us find a room. We didn't like it so sneaked out and found a nice room. Walked in town and ate at *Los Caracoles* (famous). Bought bull fight posters and saw Xmas decorations.

CALLE ESCUDILLERS, 14 - BARCELONA (ESPAÑA)

Hope the bowling party was a success!!

Dec. 17

Dear Mother & Daddy,

Arrived safely in Barcelona at 1:00 PM after a long, tiring ride. The Spanish trains are terrible (at least the one I took) - went through customs and finally got some Spanish money - 60 pesetas = $1 or 12.50 pesetas = 1 N.F.

Barcelona is a large but lovely city. The Christmas decorations are a sight to behold! Each street has its own decoration, often quite elaborate but good taste. Emily and I ate dinner here tonight. Los Caracoles means snails. I'm beginning to appreciate the amount of French that I do know. My Spanish is very bad!

Love, Barb

12/18

Walked up Avenida Santa Mónica [Plaza del Palacio – Hotel Marina]. Visited Plaza de la Universidad, Plaza de Cataluña, Plaza Monumental (bullfights & circus) – Plaza Church Sagrada Familia (intricate detail – terrible architecture) – Arco del Triunfo, Palacio de Justicia, Parque de la Ciudadela – Puerto – Paseo de Colón et Monumento a Colón.

Dinner at Amaya – then went to Pelota games (starts at 10:30). 1st game – 2 players per team = cesta, scoop. 2nd game = pala, short paddle. *Colorados y Azules* – betting - men tossed balls back and forth – betting ticket stubs inside

12/19

Tour of Barcelona – visited Cathedral, Town Hall (artist José Maria Sert), County Seat (chandelier from Venice). Poble Espanyol (Spanish town composed of replicas from all the provinces). Bought castanets and guide book to Madrid. Changed money and bought train ticket to Madrid (475 p) – left at 7:20 PM

BARCELONA
Arco de Triunfo y Palacio de Justicia.
Arc de Triomphe et Palais de Justice.
Triumphal Arc and Court of Justice.

TARJETA POSTAL

12/19

Dear Mother & Daddy,
Am having a marvelous time in Barcelona. Yesterday we walked all over the city — today we took a bus tour. Last night we went to a Pelota game (a kind of hand ball with paddles very popular in Spain). I've been very busy taking pictures. Tonight we're going to Madrid — which takes around 12 hours, ugh!
Love, Barb

POR AVION

Mr. & Mrs. W. R. And
504 Springhill Ave.
Phillips Hts.
Wilmington 3, Delaware
U. S. A.

POR AVION

12/19

Dear Mother & Daddy ,

I'm having a marvelous time in Barcelona! Yesterday we walked all over the city - today we took a bus tour.

Last night we went to a pelota game (a kind of handball with paddles - very popular in Spain). I've been very busy taking pictures. Tonight we're going to Madrid. It will take about 12 hours, ugh!

Love, Barb

12/20

Train arrived in Madrid around 9:25 AM. Walked to Avenida José Antonio – finally found a hotel, *Irureta*. Rested, then met Emily at Puerto del Sol – walked over to Plaza de España – saw statues of Don Quixote and Sancho Panza – Monument to Cervantes. Walked to Palacio Real, Plaza Oriente, Teatro Real, statue of Neptune, and Prado (bought tickets for excursions). Dinner at cafeteria (hamburger & egg).

12/21

Took excursion to Ávila, Segovia & La Granja (Cooke's), left at 8:30. Had to cross mountain roads = bad (wasn't sure we would make it).

1. Saw Ávila - old part surrounded by Roman wall, church of Santa Théresa – her special altar is supposed to be built on the same spot as the room where she was born. Monastery of Saint Thomas – tomb of [son] of Fernando & Isabella – Cathedral (big).
2. Segovia. Saw huge old Roman aqueduct still in use. Tour of Cathedral (much gold – porcelain figures of the Apostles) and big cloister. Saw Castle at Segovia – beautiful, Middle Ages.
3. La Granja. Beautiful palace. 48 fountains – copied very much after Versailles. Much snow on the way home. Enjoyed the mountains and trees covered with snow = Winter Wonderland.

501 - SEGOVIA
Vista parcial
Partial view
Vue partielle

Am having a great time taking pictures. Sure hope they...

Dec. 21

Dear Mother & Daddy,
   Today we took a tour from Madrid to Segovia where there is an old Roman aqueduct still in use!! The town is quaint & typically Spanish - I got another entirely different picture of Spanish life.
   It was very cold. We passed over the mt's. & there was a good bit of snow - but what a beautiful sight!! I saw several women washing their clothes in a river. At one place the temp was 0° below 0 - Centigrade.
                    Love, Me

Mr. & Mrs. W. R. Snow
504 Springhill Ave.
Phillips Hts.
Wilmington 3, Delaw
W. S. A.

POR AVION

I'm having a great time taking pictures. Sure hope they turn out.

Dec. 21

Dear Mother & Daddy,

   Today we took a tour from Madrid to Segovia where there is an old Roman aqueduct still in use! The town is quaint and typically Spanish. I got another entirely different picture of Spanish life.

   It was very cold. We passed over the mts. & there was a good bit of snow - but what a beautiful sight! I saw several women washing their clothes in a river. At one place the temp was 3° below 0 - centigrade.

Love, Me

12/22

<u>Toledo</u>. Left at 9:30 – met 2 American girls teaching for army in France. Saw wall and principal door of Toledo. Saw church San Juan de Los Reyes – being repaired – beautiful cloister. Jewish synagogue (roof – Lebanon wood). House of El Greco, museum. Visited Alcázar (fortress) – home of kings when Toledo was capital of Spain, then military school – terrible battle there for 72 days during Spanish Civil War.

Met Southern lady from TN, "They certainly were courageous, but then, so were we in the South!" View of old castle and Roman bridge- then view looking down on the city (3/4 surrounded by river). Visited shop where they were making objects with "Toledo gold", bought ring.

After lunch saw El Greco's famous painting *The Burial of Count Orgaz*. El Greco painted himself in the scene (only one looking out at you) – painted son – his handkerchief carried El Greco's signature and date. Saint Tomé (church). Combination of real (burial) and mystic. Visited cathedral – beautiful choir and altar. Archbishop's hat hanging about tombs. Seat of highest bishop in Spain.

12/23

Walked around Puerto del Sol, then down Calle Mayor – saw market. Went to Prado and saw mainly Spanish masterpieces.

El Greco: *La Trinidad, La Crucifixion, Bautismo de Cristo, Pentecostés*

Valázquez: *Las Hilanderas, La Rendición de Breda, Los Borrachos, Vista de Zaragoza, Las Meninas*

Guard showed me painting of Goya – court portrait painter. Also saw Tintoretto's *El Lavatorio*, Rubens' *The Three Graces*, Rafael's *La Sagrada Familia* ... Went to movie, *El Gran Pescador*, very inspiring – Howard Keel = The Big Fisherman

12/24

Walked around department stores. Saw 3 Kings who played the part of our Santa Claus. Kids told them what they wanted. Called home – real happy to talk to parents, sorry couldn't speak longer. Got them out of bed. Met an American boy in front of Prado. The 3 of us had lunch. Bought ticket and wasted time until train left.

Dear Mother & Daddy,
I'm sorry that my phone call got you out of bed. I thought it would take at least an hour, but it only took around 15 min.!

I'm going to miss you very much today & tomorrow, but we must remember that this is a chance in a lifetime. I'm really enjoying Spain. The Spaniards are much nicer than I had expected. One of the most charming places I've been is Toledo. I do hope you will decide to come to France. I would be glad to meet you in Paris. Although Spain is lovely, it will never compare to France. Love, Pat

Dec. 24

Dear Mother & Daddy,

I'm sorry that my phone call got you out of bed. I thought it would take at least an hour but it only took around 15 min!

I'm going to miss you very much today and tomorrow, but we must remember that this is a chance in a lifetime. I'm really enjoying Spain. The Spaniards are much nicer than I had expected. One of the most charming places I've been is Toledo. I do hope you will decide to come to France. I would be glad to meet you in Paris. Although Spain is lovely, it will never compare to France.

Love, Barb

12/25

Arrived in Córdoba at 6:00 AM. Walked around and found a hotel (no heat!). Slept until 11:00 AM. Walked thru downtown – very charming houses white and clean beautiful courtyards. Many orange trees. Visited Arab mosque (Mezquita). Labyrinth of columns – now Cathedral. Inside met a Spaniard who showed us around and took us up the bell tower (paid our way), beautiful view. Then another man showed us Calle de los Flores – shops and a good restaurant.

After lunch walked across the Roman bridge, then visited Alcázar, where Moorish kings lived and later Catholic kings. Combination fortress & castle – beautiful gardens, saw Moorish baths.

At night went to *El Zoco* nightclub in Jewish Quarter – saw Flamenco dancing, met 4 boys (3 from Canada and 1 from U.S.). Had very good time – boys walked us home.

12/26

Got up at 11:00 AM – went to bank, tourist office, bus depot. Walked around little streets of Córdoba. Took bus to Seville at 5:30, arrived around 9:00 PM. Found pension for 30 pt[29] a night. Ate dinner.

---

[29] Pesetas.

Dec. 26

Dear Mother & Daddy,

Córdoba is the loveliest and most atmospheric town I've seen so far. We spent Xmas Day here.

Everyone has been so friendly to us. One man showed us around the Arab mosque that is here! Another took us to his workshop and showed us his leather goods.

Last night we went to a little nightclub and saw flamenco dancing. We met 4 boys (3 from Canada and one from the US) so we had a good great time. American tourists are everywhere in Spain.

Love, Barb

12/27

Went to Cathedral – huge, but dark (not as impressive as the one in Toledo). Saw the royal chapel – relics (bones of saints), paintings, treasury (jewels, gold/silver objects). Walked around Barrio Santa Cruz – charming quaint narrow streets – white houses with beautiful courtyards, tile work, etc.

Walked thru lovely part with statue to Columbus. Visited the Alcázar – beautiful palace – fortress – saw where the harem slept. Gardens very large and beautiful. Took picture of Giralda tower. Walked down street with decorations – [Calle] Sierpes. Ate dinner at an American-style restaurant (chicken club sandwich, tea, chocolate sundae). Wrote cards, went to bed.

Dec. 27

Dear Mother & Daddy,

As you can see, I'm trying to send you a card from each place where I stop. Seville is another delightful town. The cathedral is one of the oldest in Spain.

Alcázar means fortress. This view is taken from the Alcázar toward the cathedral. Many Moorish leaders lived here. We saw the rooms where they used to keep their harems. Also the patio where they had their feasts & dancing girls! The gardens are filled with orange, lemon, & palm trees.

Tonight we found an American-type restaurant. I had a club chicken sandwich and a chocolate sundae. Didn't realize how much I enjoyed them until I ate them once again. Just think of all the food you will have to prepare for me when I come home. Ha! Ha!

Love, Barb

12/28

Walked around park María Luisa. Walked down to the Torre del Oro – 13th [century] Moslem. Walked around Barrio Triana (quaint), back to American restaurant (hamburger steak, coke, ice cream tarte).

Took bus at 7:00 for Cádiz – arrived around 9:00 PM. Went to movies with Burt Lancaster and Audrey Hepburn. Ate sandwich in café. Spent the night sleeping by park monument.

12/29

Africa is one hour ahead of Spain
500 Moroccan francs = $1.00

7:00 – after finding coffee, took bus to Algeciras and arrived at 10:00 AM. Beautiful drive thru southern Spain. Took boat at 11:20. Beautiful weather and view of Gibraltar rising majestically out of the sea. Good fortune = met an American, Bill Peddle[30], from Tangiers. He told us about it and offered to get us a cheap room.

Arrived 1:40 PM. Found a room with Bill's help. Exchanged money on black market. Bought dagger and camel charm. Then Bill showed us around and found his Arabic friend Mustafa. Showed us all around the Casba and garden of Palace. Ate dinner at Arabic restaurant, *Elias* – panchitos (liver

---

30 Presumably William Adrian Peddle, Jr. (1914-1965). Died in vehicular accident. Remains reported interred at Alcazarquivir, Morocco.

and mutton) with eggs, Jewish wine with 7UP, salad with olives, tossed salad, bread, bananas and oranges. Saw photographs of Errol Flynn when he visited there – afterwards went to bar - *Tangerie House.* Went to an Arabic movie (French subtitles). Visited a few bars - *Safari* (very atmospheric). Also bar of French girl, Tanya – sang songs.

12/30

Met Mustafa and Bill and went to see Grottoes of Hercules. Saw and rode camel (Aysha) and visited lighthouse at Cape Spartel.

Returned to Casba and ate in Mustafa's house – low couches covered with blue and silver silk. First drank <u>mint</u> tea, then couscous = large dish with wheat meal covered with chicken, almonds, grapes, and onions – delicious orange cake & mint tea. Afterwards walked all around port – saw fishing boats, contraband ships, yacht. Rode up to Marshan (European section). Drank tea in Arabic café and could see 3 lighthouses in Spain – Cádiz, Tarifa, Algeciras.

Saw Arabic funeral – no embalming or coffin. March singing with dead body thru streets, woman is wrapped in white.

Walked around Tangiers and went to restaurant *Grenouille*, visited bars – Paul Lund (former contrabander[31]) – *Carousel* – *Liaison* (piano bar run by American boys) – *Parade* (very popular too – owl & dog).

....
31 Well-known retired smuggler (1915-1966).

12/31

Met Mustafa's brother and Bill. Went to Tetouan, beautiful countryside, saw many shepherds, visited Casba and gorgeous palace (very new with modern conveniences). Bought perfume – sandalwood and jasmine. Ate in Spanish restaurant, visited Jewish Quarter, came back to Tangier.

New Year's Eve – Ate fabulous dinner at *Pous-Nice* French restaurant (ravioli niçoise, chateaubriand, tossed salad, light whipped cheese, vin rosé, bread). Went to Paul Lund's – sherry – saw him throw men out of bar. *Parade – Café Paris – Liaison – Safari* – talked with piano player (Danish Andy). Ate breakfast and went to bed at 7:30.

1/1/[1961]

Walked around town will Bill and Mustafa, saw snake charmer – after snakebite blew fire on straw. Looked for souvenirs, bought another dagger – drank mint tea and ate cookies in teahouse in Palace. Later drank tea at Mustafa's favorite bar, then dinner at *Elias*, went to Arabic movie with French subtitles, [*L'Amour sous les tenèbras*].

1/2

Bought ticket, paid bill. Had breakfast will Bill and Mustafa. Took boat ride around harbor, walked through Casba, bought teapot and good luck 5 fingered hand. Lunch at *Elias*. Man saw us down to customs and on boat. Must write to Mustafa – send him pictures and sweater from U.S. One of the best friends I will ever have – can speak 5 or 6 languages fluently – used to be a guide, now is a fisherman.

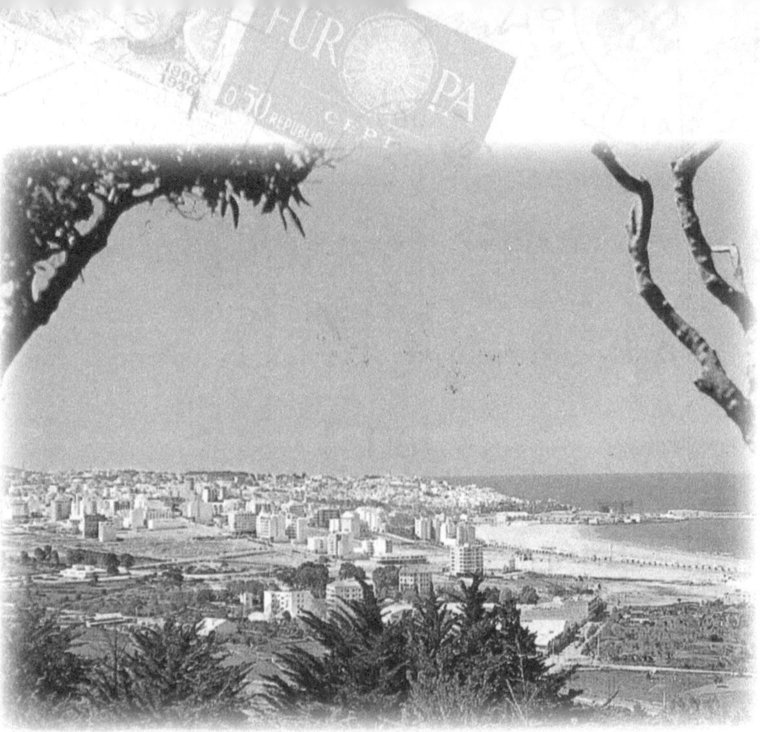

...souvenir I brought you!

TANGER - طنجة
منظر شامل للشرف
Vue générale depuis le Charf
Vista general desde el Charf
General view from the Charf

Jan. 1

Dear Mother & Daddy,
Don't worry - I'm safe well & happy - Am having a fabulous time here in Tangiers. It's a completely different fascinating world.
I've ridden a camel, seen a snake charmer, eaten a famous Arab dish called Couscous in the Casba, drunk mint-tea, & many other thrilling things.
On the way over, I met an American. He & her Arab friend have been delightful. Am leaving tomorrow for Malaga.
Love, Bert

KODACHROME S.E. PANORAMIC EDITION Reproduction Interdite

2 JAN

MAROC
10F POSTES
S.M. MOHAMED V

Mr & Mrs W. R. Snow
504 Springhill Ave
Phillips Heights
Wilmington 3, Delaw
U.S.A.

PAR AVION

PAR AVION

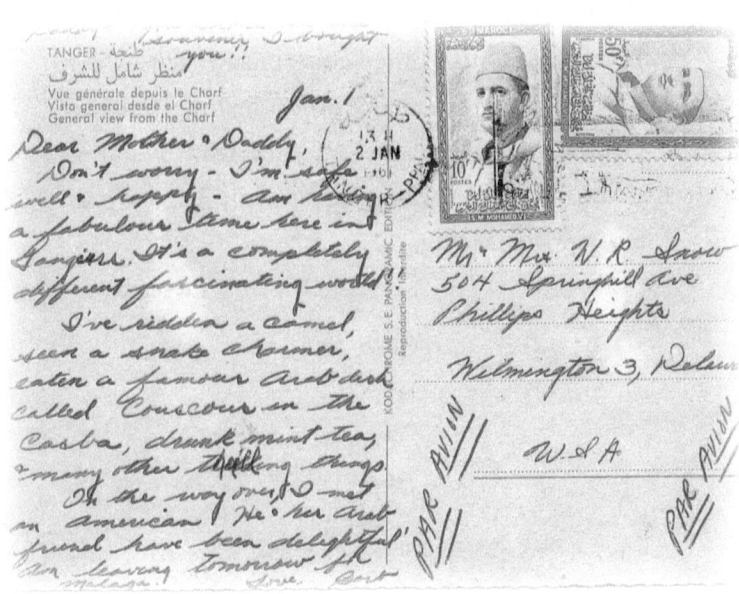

Daddy - you should see the souvenir I bought you!!

Jan. 1

Dear Mother & Daddy,

Don't worry - I'm safe, well and happy. I'm having a fabulous time here in Tangiers. It's a completely different fascinating world!

I've ridden a camel, seen a snake charmer, eaten a famous Arab dish called couscous in the Casba, drunk mint tea, and many other thrilling things.

On the way over, I met an American. He and his Arab friend have been delightful. Am leaving tomorrow for Malaga.

Love, Barb

Return To France Via Spain

On boat over, met Clint – a nice American boy in Florence, Italy with the Stanford program. Arrived at Algeciras at 7:00, bought ticket and bus at 8:00 for Málaga. Arrived around 11:00 – stayed in pension for 30 francs.

1/3

Walked around town. Lovely gardens around Alcazaba – saw women going for water and dancing. Walked along beach (no sand – big rocks). Took bus ride around city for ½ hour – delightful. Took bus at 5:00 for Granada, arrived at 9:30 PM. This time, I rented a room with heat.

1/4

Looked for tourist office and met Clint. Bought ticket to Valencia and visited Alhambra. Court of Lions, especially liked little palace that one of the Sultans built for his favorite. That night saw *Aventuras de Joselito in América*.

11 - GRANADA
Alhambra, Jardines del Partal
L'Alhambra, Jardins du Partal
The Alhambra, Gardens of the Partal

Jan. 4

Dear Mother & Daddy,

I am now safely out of Africa! Spent yesterday in Málaga which was the warmest spot I've been. Arrived last night in Granada. This is a view of a palace that one of the Sultans built for his favorite wife.

Granada was the last stronghold of the Moors in Spain. The Alhambra is very pretty, but can't possibly compare with the two Moorish palaces I saw in Africa.

Tomorrow we head for Valencia, then Barcelona, then back to Aix. Will be very happy to get back to France and my temporary home - also to read your letters.

Love, Barb

1/5

Got up at 6:00, walked to train station. Met Clint – train at 8:30 AM all day (13 hours) to Valencia – arrived 10:00. At 11:00 PM, took train to Barcelona.

1/6

Something wrong with railroad bridge. Had to stop and all passengers were transferred by buses to a station in another town. Arrived in Barcelona around 10:30 AM. Changed money and walked around town. It was a big holiday; all the kids were in the streets with the gifts which the 3 Kings had brought!

Went back to *Los Caracoles* and ate "paella" – combination of rice, fish & chicken. Had *flan au rum* - the waiter brought the dish with the rum flaming.

Took train at 2:45 – arrived at Cerbère 7:30 – French frontier. Had to wait until 10:00 for train for Marseille – good meal at station.

1/7

Arrived at Marseille at 5:00 AM – saw Clint off on train to Italy at 6:15 – took train to Aix at 7:00 and arrived around 7:45. Found heaps of letters and 4 packages waiting. Very glad to be home. Saw Georges. He was very happy with his dagger from Tangiers.

Jan. 8, 1961

Dear Mother & Daddy –

I'm back in Aix. I arrived yesterday morning and have so much to tell you that I don't know where to begin!

I'm so glad you liked the flowers. They sound lovely from your description. I was quite surprised because they gave me a choice of only red or yellow roses and that's not at all what you received. The florist here has the address of all the shops in Wilmington, so I picked Betty's hoping they would do a good job!

Also I'm very glad you like your presents. Are you sure you're telling me everything? I had a feeling that one of them would break. The lady at the antique shop will want to know if the vase arrived O.K.

When we returned we had a whole stack of letters and Christmas cards. I felt like I was having Christmas all over again hearing from everyone. I really enjoy the news more than the presents. I can't possibly tell you everyone who wrote, but here are some: Aunt Esther, Mrs. Morton (a lovely letter), Mrs. Todd, Ed (I didn't send him anything, ha! ha!), Miss Stewart, Mrs. Davis, Carol Hoffecker[32], the Crawfords (no letter), Aunt Bertha, Lorrie, Nancy[33], Ruth (the girl who went to Ocean City last summer with us) and of course the usual people. I saved yours and Roberta's letters until the last! I always like to save the best, you know.

Here is some gossip. Nancy and Berch are depinned. I must say I think it's for the best! Nancy Walton is going to have a baby this spring. Lorrie has finally reached her goal - she is engaged and plans to marry this summer. Eleanor and Nancy [are] both are planning to come to Europe next summer (not together).

After reading the letters and sleeping, I dashed off to the post office and the R.R. station to collect no less than 4 packages! Glady sent me a beautiful red sweater (mazet), Aunt Ruby sent me a lovely white drip-dry blouse with light blue embroidery. Kathy sent me a dainty white nightshirt that I can use this summer. Of course I am delighted beyond words with your package. The sweater is absolutely beautiful and goes so well with the skirt. The skirt looks very nice; it's a bit loose, but not too much. You know how I hate tight skirts. Thank goodness

---

32 Classmate at Mount Pleasant High School and University of Delaware.

33 Classmates at the University of Delaware.

it is short enough - that still seems to be my main clothing problem! The hose are really needed. I wash a pair every day, but they don't seem to last very long.

Also the nightshirt is very much needed. I think I don't dare bring the others home for you to see! Thank you so much. I feel as though I don't deserve all these nice things!! The camera case also arrived and fits beautifully. I took 4 rolls of film over the vacation. I just hope they turn out! Sue Ellen sent me a pair of stockings. I think I told you before that Grandmother sent pants, and Waltine & Denis pajamas for summer. Roberta sent a lovely blouse and charm (Christmas tree).

It sounds as though your Christmas vacation consisted mainly of going to functions for Margie's wedding! I think it's a shame they couldn't have done with less functions and have a longer honeymoon. Roberta sent me a clipping and picture. Margie certainly did look lovely! She has so much style! What color were her bridesmaids dresses and what kind of flowers did they carry? Who got the bouquet? Was the dinner as nice as the Stephensons'? I'm sure you both looked very nice and stylish - you always do. I never have to worry about how my parents look!

Well, I think I had one of the most delightful vacations imaginable! Although I didn't speak

Spanish very well, I can understand a good bit, and I think we got along fabulously. Of course, Emily had spent 3 months in Mexico last winter. The Spanish people are very friendly and always delighted to help you, especially 2 young girls. All you have to do is ask! You won't believe this, but we didn't carry suitcases. They're so cumbersome. Instead, we each carried a little sack over our shoulders. For 3 weeks, I wore the same 2 sweaters and the same 2 skirts. Of course that made 4 different outfits! Also took my wrinkle-resistant blue dress. The places we stayed were not the greatest and we usually ate only one big meal a day, but we really got an education.

We learned much about the people and how to get around. I detest [how the Spanish men] hiss at you all the time. Hissing means they are trying to flirt with you. They are much too friendly and I told several where to go!

You can tell by my cards pretty much our itinerary: Barcelona, Madrid, Córdoba, Seville, Algeciras, Tangiers, Málaga, Granada, and back to Barcelona. The American Express office was closed when I came back through, so I guess I'll have to write for my mail.

Hope you weren't worried about Morocco. It has been independent now for 4 or 5 years. They have their own king, money, laws, etc. Tangiers was a completely new world for me. I'd love to learn Arabic! It is a very rich country and probably will have a prosperous future. I will write you all about it in my next letter!

I'm very glad to get back with my friends. Georges was pleased with the dagger I bought him in Tangiers. I will find out about Easter vacation next week.

Love,
Barb

Jan. 9

Dear Mother & Daddy-

Well here I go again - expounding about my trip! As I said before, Morocco is a completely new world, very beautiful and exotic. We took the boat over from Algeciras - no problems. Its sails every day except Sunday. By some great stroke of luck, I met an American, about 40 years old, who has lived in Africa for the last 7 years and is now residing in Tangiers. He said he would be glad to get us an inexpensive room and show us around. Well for 5 days, he hardly left us! At the end I was getting quite angry because we wanted some time to explore for ourselves, but we were fortunate to meet him. He was out of work - rather timid - the harmless type. I actually think he got a great bang out of showing us around.

He has an Arab friend who actually lives in the Casba, called Mustafa. We both fell in love with him immediately. He too is a little old for us so there were no problems. I've never met such a delightful person! He can speak 5 or 6 languages fluently, used to be an interpreter, and also a guide. Now he is in the fishing business. He wears modern clothes. Although he can speak these languages well, the only one he can read is Arabic. All the signs of the country are written in French and Arabic. You should see Coca-Cola, 7-Up, Pepsi Cola, etc. written in Arabic. As you can see I was in Pepsi Cola paradise both in Spain and Morocco! The fishing business was slow so Mustafa was with us most of the time.

You should see the Casba! It is built on the side of the hill. Many of the women still cover their faces. The men also wear long robes often. Most of them are poor. Mustafa took us to a delightful restaurant in the Casba; we went there several times. The cooking [here] was superior to Spanish cuisine.

One day we went on a tour of the land outside the city and saw many shepherds with their flocks. We both rode on a camel - believe me, it's not easy! We also saw underground caves and went up in a lighthouse. Spain is very visible from Tangiers.

The highlight of the whole vacation I think was the day Mustafa invited us to his home in the Casba. Inside it was very nice and clean. We sat on low couches covered with a colorful silk fabric. First we drank green mint tea, which is absolutely delicious. Then the couscous - this is also popular in France - it's an Arab dish. It is a sort of meal made with wheat. You can put on top of the mound of meal either chicken or mutton. We had chicken. Mixed in were also large raisins, almonds, and fried onions which had most of their taste.

For dessert we had delicious orange cake and more mint tea. The women of the house did not eat with us, but we managed to thank them before we left.

Also we saw some beautiful Arab palaces. We went to 2 Arab movies with French subtitles fortunately. I'm quite fascinated and would just love to learn Arabic. I now know 3 words, ha! Maybe if I go to graduate school someday I can take it. One day we also went to Tétouan, not far from Tangiers. Also interesting. Just before we left, Mustafa took us on a boat ride of the harbor.

The American, Bill Peddle, took us to delightful restaurants and nightclubs several nights. I met a fascinating man who used to deal with contraband. Tangiers is not as popular with the contraband ships as it used to be before their independence. Uncle Sam Heltzel[34] would really have loved this man!

Mustafa and Bill took us down to the boat, saw us through customs, and waved us off. I really hated to leave! I asked him if there was anything

---

34 Samuel Clinton Heltzel, Jr. (1912-1982).

he particularly wanted from France, but he's quite interested in the US. He's very proud of a sweater he has from the US. I wondered if maybe sometime soon, you could buy a pretty sweater (he has blue) - about medium size and send it to him along with a thank you note for giving me such a good time. He can get Bill to translate the note. I know he would really appreciate it. Here is his address:

> Rue Tapiro
> c/o Café Deportivo
> Tanger, Morocco

We spent Christmas night in a nightclub in Córdoba and saw Flamenco dancing. New Year's Eve, we were doing the town in Tangiers - didn't get to bed until 7:00 in the morning!!

Spring vacation here is from March 26 to April 9. I would be delighted to have you both come, or just you, Mother. Of course, without Daddy your budget may be a little limited, but Emily and I have been doing alright. I only have 5 checks left so I thought maybe you could send me some money for my birthday! I could use it for spring vacation and this summer. I'm definitely going to try to make it to Italy over spring vacation, but this time I'd like to spend a more restful vacation! Maybe just Florence, Pisa, and Rome. I wish Georges would come along, but I doubt he would be able!

Here are 2 pictures of me. They aren't very good but at least you can see that I'm well and happy!

Love, Barb

Jan. 19

Dear Mother & Daddy,

Sorry I haven't written sooner. I've been a little under the weather and just didn't feel like writing when I didn't feel well. At any rate, I am much better now.

I'm afraid I'm going to get an attack of homesickness one of these days. I was too busy to think during Christmas vacation, but at last the merry-go-round has slowed down! Also Georges is getting to be a bit of problem. He thinks he loves me and is afraid of the future so he thinks we should not see each other for awhile. Well, I realize we both might be a little sad when I leave to go home, but why complicate matters now? Besides he is the romantic & moody type. Not seeing each other will be a new adventure of him. Honestly, men are the same the world over I think!

I bought a card with roses for [Great] Aunt Katy[35]. Does she have any friends in the nursing home?

....

35 Martha Catherine Heatwole Swope (1870-1964) lived in the Virginia Mennonite Home in Harrisonburg, Virginia.

I feel as though I'm missing out on all the Kennedy doings. I'm so glad his brother finally decided to be Attorney General. Maybe you can send me a list of the other cabinet members sometime.

Dear Mother, I'm sorry to hear that you can't make it over. I really think you should make every effort! You know how much you've always wanted to see Europe. Just think you would be able to see Paris in the Springtime. Frankly, I don't see that there is much trouble getting ready to come if you don't have a trunk. If you get that economical T.W.A. round-trip ticket, you pay about $315. After your ticket, get a passport (you'll need a few pictures which you should do anyway) and then only 1 shot for smallpox. Clothes should be absolutely no problem. If I can wander around Spain & Tangiers with 2 outfits (for 3 weeks), you can certainly manage with a suitcase. Daddy can take you to New York and I'll meet you in Paris.

Well I hope that doesn't sound like a sales talk, but I'm sure you've had no encouragement. There's absolutely nothing frightening about coming. You should see all the Americans I've met. As far as any trip to Italy, I would prefer it to be leisurely this time. Although we had a fabulous time, I was really tired out. Also Emily is quite a fanatic at saving money. I'm afraid if I don't have a certain amount of comfort, I will not be too happy. We stayed at different hotels once or twice during the trip. I got to the point where I had to have heat and warm water.

I didn't call collect from Spain because it can't be done there, so maybe I shall call another time - this time - collect from France...

You haven't heard about my souvenirs. I want to see Daddy's face when he sees what I brought from Tangiers so I suppose you'll have to wait, Dad. Mother, I bought you a change purse for the grocery money; it's made from the famous leather from Córdoba. I also bought some castanets - the little things the Spanish girls snap when they dance. In Tangiers, I bought a little silver teapot and also some exotic perfume. I received in the mail from Marvin and Virginia[36] a lovely engagement calendar of the US with a different scene for each week.

....

36 Marvin Bryan Miller (1924-2002) and Virginia Mae Bowman Miller (1924-2006).

I forgot to ask about Margie's ring. Was it a double ring ceremony?

Well that's about all my news. This afternoon I've been invited to a French girl's room for tea so I think that will be very nice. Another girl coming will be Jaqueline Olagnon, the daughter of Dr. St. Aubryn's friend.

Love,
Barb

CAFE DEPORTIVO
RUE TAPIRO N° 1
TANGER
MOROCCO

24 JAN. 1961

Dear Mr. and Mrs. Snow –

Your very kind letter was received and read to me by Mr. Peddle who comes to my Cafe quite frequently – I only read and write Arabic but speak English as well – We both appreciate your letter and had an interesting time showing Barbara and Carolyn around Tanger and Tetuan.

Thanks for your invitation to visit you in Wilmington should either of us be able to do so – We appreciate the thoughtfulness of you both.

If you would like any sort of souvenir from Tanger – just write me and I will send something.

Please send best regards to Barbara and Carolyn.

Sincerely,

MUSTAFA BONAZA (and Bill Peddle)

P.S. If any of your friends come to Tanger, send them to see me and I will be glad to show them the sights.

Jan. 24

Dear Mother & Daddy –

So nice to hear from you. It certainly is a shame about Mrs. Hartmann.

You only sent me one package didn't you? The station sent me notice of another one. The duty on it was expensive so I was rather happy when they couldn't find it; however, if you did send another one, I will investigate further. The camera case fits fine.

I have received most of my slides now. They are really good if I do say so myself. Wait until you see me perched on top of a camel! Thanks so much for buying the sweater for Mustafa. I'm sure he will love it.

The other night at the Franco-Anglo club, we ate a special cake, *gâteau des rois*. Whoever found a bean was king or queen. He or she then chose a partner. I was quite honored when one of my French friends chose me to be his queen!

I'm still having problems with Georges. I'm getting sick of the whole thing now and am about ready to tell him where to go!!

I went to see the movie, *Mein Kampf,* a story of Hitler. It was very informative but frightful. I also saw *From the Terrace* again. Only this time, Paul Newman speaks French!! You can imagine the feeling I had when I saw the sign, "Wilmington, 5 miles".

I made a delightful purchase Saturday. I finally bought an <u>iron</u>. I didn't want to worry you, but I have not been able to use mine. The current at Mme Roman's was changed just last year. The iron I bought is very good and works on both currents, so I am ecstatically happy!

I bought 2 bullfight posters while in Spain, but I guess you don't want another one do you, Daddy?

Thanks for speaking to Mrs. Wyatt. In a way, I would like to go to graduate school, but I suppose that can wait a year. Teaching will be a good experience – providing I can find a job.

Love,
Barb

February 4

Dear Mother & Daddy –

It is really hard to believe that the weather is so cold in Delaware! It would have to pick the winter I'm away to snow! The weather here gets cold at times but nothing like that. There have been some days when the sun is very bright - then it almost looks like spring. I can unbutton my coat. The sky is a beautiful medium blue with white puffy clouds. Of course, there are other days when it really feels like winter, especially when the wind blows.

At the cooking class last Saturday, we make crêpes, something like *Crêpes Suzette*. They are very light pancakes. We folded them and put jelly inside. They seem to be quite popular this time of year - around Mardi Gras.

We just had a fabulous time in Grenoble last weekend!! Emily, Jackson, Diana, and I rode up in Diana's car. Cathie has a lovely roommate. I think I'm rather envious. She was so happy to see us. Lois's place is not very nice, but she has a darling French roommate which makes up for that quite a lot. I sent you a souvenir from Grenoble and let me know if it arrives. Cathie and Lois may come down to visit us next before too long.

Everyone here is talking about the Mardi Gras. We get 5 days off from school. The carnival in Aix begins today and is to last for around 2 weeks. They say there will be times when we can't cross the main street without paying a fare. At least it should be exciting!!

Diana and I and probably Emily (with us) are going visiting during the holidays. Diana and I plan to leave the evening of the 10th. Emily is leaving earlier, of course, but we may meet her. We hope to visit Monte Carlo on the 11th. On the 12th we plan to visit the orange festival in Menton. (You can trace these cities on the map.) The 13th, we will return to Monte Carlo or Monaco. The 14th, we will be in Nice for the actual Mardi Gras festivities. We plan to stay also the 15th and 16th. On the 16th, they're having the Second Battle of Flowers. Diana and I are then coming back to Aix.

I don't believe I've told you yet. My reservations are made for coming home!! I will be sailing from Le Havre on the <u>S.S. United States</u> July 27, and I should arrive in New York on July 31. I do hope you can keep this day in mind as I expect you to give me the royal welcome home! I wanted to try a different ship this time. The <u>Flandre</u> doesn't sail at the end of July so I chose this one first and the <u>Liberté</u> second.

Did you ever receive the pictures of me in Spain? I sent one that was taken in El Greco's house and another in the Pueblo Español. They're not particularly good, but you can see how healthy I look. Recently I've lost a little weight, but I will probably gain it back soon unfortunately. Since the new student restaurant opened, I really have a way to go. It takes between 20 and 25 minutes.

Emily and I made a delightful purchase yesterday. We bought a hot plate, so now we can have coffee, tea, chocolate, soup, etc. in our room.

I'm so glad you heard from Mustafa. I plan to write this weekend. I just can't get caught up on my letter writing. Emily and I are going to send Mustafa and Bill some pictures made from our slides if we ever get them back.

Tonight I'm going to a ball. I feel a bit odd since I don't have the date. One of my friends asked me if I were coming. When he found out that I wasn't coming, he insisted that I sit with him and his friends at their table. Some of his friends will be without dates. One of the boys is the one who chose me as his queen that night at the Franco-Anglo club. Maybe I will meet someone interesting and forget about Georges.

M. Ruff's wife is having us early next Wednesday night for refreshments, probably because of the carnival festivities.

No I haven't been studying very hard. I'm beginning to study more now, but it is such a chore to fit in sometimes and just do the everyday things so easy at home!

Yes, I don't know all of those nurses in the newspaper clipping you sent. They look quite successful, don't they? I sent Kathy a card.

Love, Barb

Côte d'Azur

2/10

Left Aix at 4:45 with Diana – Emily – Jack. Went to Fréjus – then over by way of coast - took Jack home at Nice. 8:30 ate dinner at Nice then found hotel in Beausoleil, suburb of Monte Carlo.

2/11

Visited the Place de Palace – walked around gardens. Saw church where Grace [Kelly] was married. Visited Oceanography Museum – excellent, all sorts of fish, bones of whales, whaling ship and weapons, instruments, etc. Walked back to Palace and took pictures of Monte Carlo & Port across the way. Ate, then went over to the Casino, sat by water (can see <u>Italy</u> from here). Walked down to the wharf, then looked at ships, changed clothes and went to Casino. Played slot machines and roulette wheel. 5 NF a chip – played one chip and saved other for souvenir.

2/12

Rode over to Menton. Visited Vieux Port and city, sat in sun, saw Parade at 3:00 – floats made out of oranges and lemons – confetti everywhere! Saw *La Salle des Mariages* in City Hall – decorated by Jean Cocteau. Saw movie with Marilyn Monroe and Yves Montand (*Let's Make Love*). Rode over to Ventimiglia for dinner. The scenery is out of this world!!

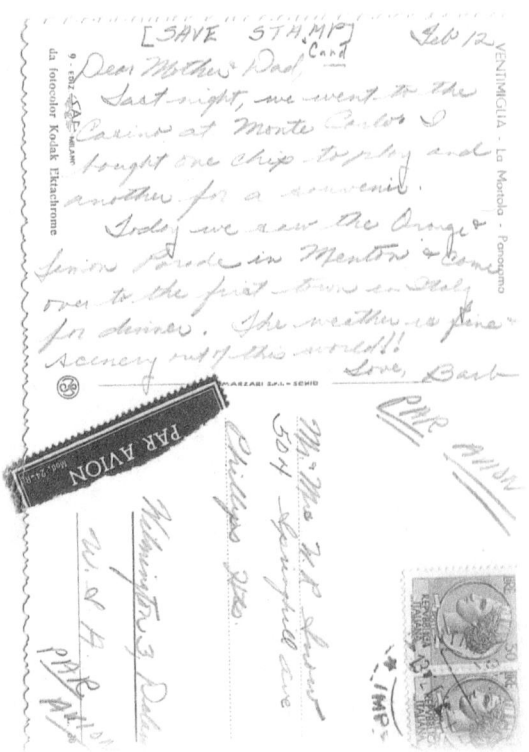

Feb. 12

Dear Mother & Dad,

 Last night we went to the casino at Monte Carlo. I bought one chip to play and another for a souvenir. Today we saw the Orange and Lemon Parade in Menton and came over to the first town in Italy for dinner. The weather is fine and scenery out of this world!!

Love, Barb

2/13

Walked to Vieux Port and lighthouse then around the *Quai des Etats-Unis* and up mountainside to Monaco – ate picnic – lunch in the gardens overlooking the sea. Then visited the exotic gardens and grottoes. Saw 4 German friends.

Then visited La Turbie – Roman monument built to commemorate the subjugation of the Gaulic tribes in this area, built to honor Augustus in 5 BC. Beautiful panoramic view of Monaco and Monte Carlo. Rode to Roquebrune to see old château. Visited lovely shop where man makes olive wood bowls, boards, etc. by hand.

2/14

Went back to La Turbie and then to Nice by [Grande] Corniche. Finally found a place (Villa Josephine) – walked down Promenade des Anglais, met Jacques at 2:15 – saw Parade and was quite impressed (high floats and many horses). Confetti all over the place! After the Parade, we walked down the Promenade and then up to the Château to see sunset, then around the Port. Ate 2 typical niçoise dishes: *La Socca* and *La Pissaladière*.

Met Jacques' father and brother – ate dinner near other Fulbrights (*Cyrano*) then saw the *feux d'artifices*[37] (beautiful and elaborate). Then we rode back to the Place Masséna to see the decorations again – more confetti!!

---

37 Fireworks.

2/15

Met Jacques at his home at 11:00. Also met mother and sister (lovely family). Stayed on beach until 2:45 – beautiful weather, picked 2 stones, then rode to Villefranche and saw Chapelle St. Pierre now designed by Cocteau. Saw church and port, Then to Èze – delightful ancient city built on side of hill (can easily tell the Arab influence). Beautiful view and ate lemon meringue pie – 1 piece for 4. Let Jacque off on way back. Ate dinner again at *Cyrano*.

Feb. 15

Dear Mother & Dad,

Here we are at Nice! Our French friend has been quite lovely. He is a wonderful guide!! We actually spent some time on the beach today although it's too cold to go swimming!

Yesterday we saw the Mardi Gras Parade which was quite impressive! Tomorrow we are going to see the Second Battle of Flowers and then Diana, Jacque (our friend) and I are heading back to Aix. It was worth the trip to Europe just to see most of the towns on the Riviera. I feel as though I'm in a fairy land.

Love, Barb

[2]/16

Dropped Emily off at the Joyaux – bought food, stamps, ate lunch on the beach. Picked Jacque up and saw *Seconde Bataille des Fleurs* (very beautiful flowers, girls, music). Girls threw flowers and the crowd threw them back. Then went to Vence – Chapel Matisse and Les Galerie d'Arts - Grasse. Left Emily's suitcase at Jacque's – St. Cristophe. Got home around 1:00 AM.

Feb. 18

Dear Mother & Daddy –

It was so good to hear from you when I got home. The only letters waiting for me were yours. I guess Roberta and Glady are busy with their schoolwork. Thank you so much for the valentine and the money (Roberta did send me a valentine). I've been wanting to buy a suede jacket - that's what the best-dressed girls seemed to be wearing so I think I'll put the money in a jacket fund!

Also thank you so much for the $200. I will try not to use it until July. We get paid until the end of June. I'm very glad that I don't have to cash it all at once. It was very clever of you, Daddy, to have them find out the name of my bank. Some kids seem to have a lot of trouble cashing checks.

The pictures of you and the snow seem very exciting to me since we don't have snow here! I've been showing them to my friends.

The first bulletin from the placement bureau indicates several interesting jobs - one in Pennsylvania and several in New Jersey (I don't really think much of New Jersey). However, the New Castle administration wrote saying they were very much interested in me and I would be hearing from them soon. Also since they have my credentials they could send me a contract without my having another interview. I think I will wait awhile since I prefer New Castle. I'm really not interested in working, but I guess this delightful life I'm leading will eventually come to an end.

Well, my trip to the Riviera was the best yet! I'm convinced that the French Riviera is the most beautiful spot in the whole world. They not only have the most beautiful blue water, but lots of mountains too. You can visit the fairly large and modern cities like Cannes or Nice or you can go to a darling little quaint village like Villafranche, Èze, or even Menton. The orange and lemon parade in Menton was lovely, but not nearly as good as the parade here in Aix. Of course, the best is in Nice. The only disturbing thing is the confetti. It is sold for 20¢ a bag and everyone throws it. You should see the streets after everything is over! Some of the men and older boys come up from behind and force it in your mouth!! It is very exhausting. I had to buy several bags to defend myself.

The *Bataille des Fleurs* is the best, in my opinion. The floats are works of art with beautiful flowers and lovely girls. Often horses are pulling them. Romantic music is played and the floats parade up and down the *La Promenade des Anglais,* the main Street in Nice by the sea. It's called a battle because the girls throw flowers at the crowd, and the crowd throws them back. I kept the two flowers that I caught. Jacque, our French friend, was a delightful guide. He showed us all around Nice and saw that we ate two dishes that are typically niçoise. We also met his family who are lovely people. His father upholsters and repairs furniture. We met several Fulbright kids from Poitiers, but I never found Cathie and Lois.

Emily went off to visit the brother of her French professor, and we never saw her again. She is the most selfish and inconsiderate person I've yet to meet! Jacque, Diana, and I had to drive all the way to Grasse, then look for a friend's home which took several hours before we found it. We knew Emily was going to meet this friend today in Grasse and I wanted to leave her suitcase. I am determined that I'm not going to Italy with her if there's any way possible. Since I don't know the language and the Italians are famous for cheating tourists, I'm going to try to join an organized tour. That way your traveling, sightseeing, and lodging are all taken care of. I imagine I would probably meet some interesting people on the tour. Organized tours are not always the best way to see a city or a country, but I think I'll try it anyway.

Monaco and Monte Carlo seem just like a fairyland. I took lots of pictures. I've saved my roulette chip for you, Daddy. Also collected two rocks from Nice. We visited a lovely little town called La Turbie where there is still standing a Roman monument commemorating the defeat of the southern French tribes by Augustus. I bought two modern ceramic vases and an olive wood dish for hors-d'oervres.

I think I will try to call you "collect" on my birthday if that's agreeable.

The weather has been out of this world! We wore our bathing suits on the beach at Nice. The water is still cold. Here at Aix, I've started wearing my car-coat. The almond trees are all in blossom. They are the first flowers here; however, I've seen a few iris and daffodils on the Riviera.

Tomorrow the Fulbrights have been invited to Cassis, a lovely the little town near Marseille for dinner (we pay) and a tour of some exotic gardens.

Did you fill out an income tax form for me, Daddy? Didn't I tell you how much money they owe me?

Love,
Barb

THE CASINO CHIP BARBARA GAVE TO HER FATHER.
HE KEPT IT IN MIND CONDITION.[38]

．．．．．．．．．．．．．．．．．．．

38 In return, Barbara's father bought her a souvenir chip from a trip to Las Vegas. Barbara kept this chip in her wallet to be with her always and, as a result, it became worn.

L-R: Diana, Jacques [?], Barbara

Feb. 23

Dear Mother & Daddy –

I have not heard from anyone this week after I took all that trouble to send postcards from my trip. Well, at least this way, I won't have to worry about answering them. Yesterday I received a nice letter from Aunt Trene[39]!!

Have you received anything from Grenoble yet? It's about time you did.

I wonder if you could find out how much a 1/4 of an ounce of Lanvin perfume is. On the trip, I bought 4 little bottles for $8.90. It seems like a good buy. I think I will send Kathy a bottle and a bar of perfumed soap from Spain for a birthday present.

You might be interested in that food we have at the University restaurant. We have a new restaurant now which is quite large. Two sides are all glass windows. The meals are about 25¢ each. For lunch we have an hors d'oeuvre like small pieces of lunch meat with olives, pizza, sardines (which

---

39 Trene Rebecca Heltzel King (1910-1995).

I have learned to like - their heads have been removed). Then we have a meat dish, usually some kind of beef - sometimes pork - fish on Friday. For vegetables we often have rice or macaroni with cheese, potatoes (their French fries are delicious), peas, beans, cooked celery, etc. Sometimes we have a green salad - lettuce or endive.

Dessert it's always a fruit (oranges at least once a day) and cookies. Dinner is the same except we always begin with soup and finish with fruit and cheese. Also there is plenty of bread and water. I usually have coffee or chocolate later at a café. I think the food is far superior to anything I ever ate at [the University of] Delaware except we don't have the desserts.

Last Friday night Diana and I went to a play given here at Aix by the Comédie française - one of the best groups at Paris. It was a modern play by Anouilh[40]. It was rather good although more difficult to understand that some. After I read the program, it was much easier to comprehend.

Sunday we went to a darling little port town near Marseille. The Fulbrights were invited by former French Fulbright students. There is an organized group in Marseille, and they have arranged

---

40 Jean Marie Lucien Pierre Anouilh (1910-1987). The play was *L'Hurluberlu*.

some kind of excursion for us each month. We had to pay for our dinner - 10 NF or $2, ugh! Then we visited the private gardens (exotic) and wine cellar of the grandfather of one of the girls in the association.

Saturday night Diana came over and we cooked ravioli on our hot plate! It was great fun!

The Fulbright association has gotten free tickets for us to go to the opera at Marseille tomorrow night! I may go early and stop at the American Embassy. I would like to find out about sending my trunk home in June. If I am touring around, I hate to have it to worry about that too.

We received a letter from Bill and Mustafa this week. They have been happy to hear from us and Mustafa's sweater fits fine, they say. We are in the process of getting some pictures made from some slides (about 5) for them.

Well I bought my jacket and I'm thrilled with it! It is dark brown suede. It can be worn for other things as well as sporting occasions. I paid a little too much for it so you're $10 is really helpful while I await the arrival of my next check.

Saturday I'm going on an excursion with one of my classes to a château, monastery, and ancient tower not too far from here although the excursion will take all day. I think he (the professor) will eventually take us to see the *Pont du Gard*. If not,

I'll go myself. Camus is buried in one of the little villages we will be passing through.

Sunday will be another exciting day, I'm going with a group by airplane to Corsica. We will only be in Bastia for a few hours, but I'm really excited about the plane. The trip has been organized by Air France. The cost of the trip is about $12 to go and come. I think the ride will be worth that for me. Diana is going too.

As you say, I have not been killing myself studying this year; however, I do go to some great classes. My translation paper was the second best in the class the other day. But I can't be too boastful since Georges helped me some, although some of the other kids have help too, I know. I don't plan to take the exams at the end. Very few Fulbrights do. I would have to spend all my time studying for the courses, and I've been reading and studying some books and authors that I always wanted to know. For instance I know something about André Gide now and I've read three books by Camus. You know Camus just died last year. About a week before the accident, he came to the Institute and spoke for 3 hours. I surely wish I could have seen him.

I heard on the Voice of America the other night that the US is having another business recession.

Things don't sound too hopeful. I'm beginning to think Kennedy got in just in time! Everyone over here is kidding us (Americans) about Germany lending us money. The prestige of the US has certainly gone up since the election. Maybe it's because he has a French wife – ha! ha!

Love,
Barb

March 1

Dear Mother & Daddy,

Things are rather quiet this week, but I suppose I can tell you about last weekend.

Friday I went into Marseille during the afternoon. I didn't get too much accomplished. After I went to the consulate, I had to find a company that is managing all the American Express affairs now. It was closed by the time I arrived. At any rate, I can send the trunk home, but it may be necessary for someone to take it through customs for me. Do you think you could do that?

Friday night I went with the other Fulbrighters to the opera in Marseille. We saw *La Chauve-Souris* by Strauss[41]. The music was delightful although I find it hard to really appreciate opera. Perhaps it's because I never studied it.

Saturday I went on an excursion with one of my classes. We saw an old monastery (*L'Abbaye de Silvacane*) built in the 12th and 15th centuries. It was quite interesting. I think our teacher took

---

41 *Die Fledermaus.*

us into every [nook] and cranny he could find. He really loves this sort of work.

We ate lunch (provençal cuisine) - very delicious - at a charming little town called Lourmarin. Camus lived here and we saw his grave. I took two pictures of it! Then we went to the famous castle there built in the 15th or 16th century. Famous artists and writers come here in the summer to work. After Lourmarin, we visited another château in Ansouis. You would have really loved the antiques in these two places, mother.

Well Sunday, I finally got to ride in an airplane - Air France. I was a little disappointed that it wasn't a jet, but it only takes about 50 minutes from Marignane (near Marseille) to Bastia, Corsica. Our plane had 4 engines. The hostess was very lovely and sweet. They gave us candy and served apéritifs and sandwiches.

Everything looks so different in the air. You just can't imagine how excited I was when the airplane took off. I thought to myself, I don't particularly want to die, but I can't think of a better way to go!! The trip was very smooth. Coming home at night we saw the sunset and then the lights down below! The only thing that bothered me was coming down. I had a little cold in my head, nothing noticeable; but I got this terrible pain over my right eye. Poor Diana had a terrible time with her ears. She said with all the times she has flown in the States, she never felt anything like that. At any rate, I was fine when we landed. I was also surprised to see how easily we landed. I expected a big bang!

Well, the plane ride was the reason I went. Corsica is lovely - high mountains of snow and beautiful seashore, but I will always prefer the French Riviera. We ate lunch in Bastia and then walked around town seeing the sights. I got lost for about ½ hr. I really had a delightful trip.

Tuesday night some of us went to a show here in Aix of Spanish dancers. They were very good-beautiful costumes too! I prefer the Flamenco of all the dances. Emily and I saw some of that at Córdoba during Christmas.

My plans for Easter are a bit unsettled. Diana now thinks she might like to go and maybe see a little bit of Greece. I'm waiting for her to decide!

I feel as though you have already given me enough for my birthday; however, I could use more stockings and another girdle. If you get a girdle, I would like to have one exactly like I have now -Maidenform - medium – Fris-Kee. I need another summer skirt, but perhaps I can pick something up in Italy.

I wore my jacket to Corsica. I just am thrilled to death with it! Diana took a picture of me in it.

I see by the paper I buy once in awhile that spring training has started. It's going to be very hard thinking of Leo Durocher as a Dodger coach or manager, which is it? I suppose you've seen the cover of *Look* magazine, February 28. Kennedy and family. I have one here, but perhaps you can save one for me at home. I have a lovely bunch of daffodils (10) in my room now. I bought them at the market for 20¢. I'm getting rather hungry for pickled eggs[42], but I guess I'll just have to wait.

I was so sorry to learn of the King of Monaco's death. Most people seem to really like him.

Love, Barb.

PS – Glad to hear that Daddy is doing so well bowling.

Mme Roman's phone number is 14-19.

---

42 A Pennsylvania Dutch (German) dish that Barbara always made at Easter and which her son detested!

Diana [?] in front of airplane to Corsica

PHOTO OF BARBARA IN THE SUEDE JACKET

March 6

Dear Mother & Daddy –

I just received your letter of March 2 in the mail. The mail seems to be back to normal by now. I certainly did not mean that I had not been hearing enough from you. You write even better than I do, and I really enjoy hearing from you even if your letter is short.

Roberta did write too this week. That poor child is so wrapped up in her work that I don't think she could possibly carry on a normal conversation without interjecting her job every other minute. Her letter was one big rundown of her school activities. She really is getting duller instead of more interesting. I think, myself, that one should do his job as best as he possibly can, but life has much more to offer, and Roberta certainly isn't taking advantage of it. Perhaps she has a romantic interest, but just didn't tell me about it.

I'm afraid you both think I'm very lazy this year and I am having all fun and no work. Well, in a sense this is true. I've never spent such a wonderful year in my life, but it has not all been a bowlfull of cherries. There are several reasons why I don't plan to take the exams. First of all, I would not get any credit in the States. The most I could possibly get would be 4 or 6 credits (2 courses) from Middlebury & I have decided that I'm going to try for Yale or North Carolina (next year, of course). Secondly, to take an exam, I would have to follow <u>all</u> the civilization courses or all the literature courses. You can't take an exam for each course the way we do! I frankly don't think this would be worth it. Some of the French professors are very dull and uninteresting. The vast majority of them read their entire lecture from their notes. I could learn as much, or more, if I read a book on my own. M. Ruff and a few others do actually discuss with us and interject their own personalities. However, M. Ruff has taught in England and the States.

Thirdly, I just don't have that much time to study. I think my French improves most by conversing with my French friends. I also have some wonderful English and American friends. We have some delightful discussions. Most of the kids are much more interesting than those were at college. At any rate, I feel as though I know much more about life now. I certainly have been living more actively than before. I hope you don't think I sound like a stuffy intellectual. Believe me, more than ever, I am realizing how little I know. I love France, but I'm sure I won't miss it as much as I'll miss all my friends.

Of course there's a chance that I will see the Americans again. Cricket, Jackson, Diana, and maybe Lois will be at the University of North Carolina next year. Yes, I like Diana very much. I don't agree with her always, but we seem to fit together. She is from Arkansas. Jackson is [from] Virginia or North Carolina. Cricket is from Virginia and North Carolina too.

The cooking course Saturday was another big success. We made cannelloni, a green bean dish, and *Omelette au Rhum*. Cannelloni is something like a huge noodle. You spread a filling (chicken, beef or fish etc.) on it and then roll it up and bake it. The green beans were mixed with carrots, potatoes, and an aioli sauce. Aioli is a mixture of mayonnaise, olive oil, and garlic. It's much better than it sounds. The omelette was made like an ordinary omelette. Then we put jelly on it and folded it over. Then added sugar and rum. It flamed when we lit it with a match.

Saturday night I went to a concert of Beethoven music. I enjoyed it although I know very little about good music. I did enjoy the pianist very much. He was an old man with white hair, but could he do those trills!

Yesterday, Jackson, Jean Kinnon (my friend from England) and I went on a picnic. We walked out into the country. The sun is very warm from 11:00 to 4:00. We plopped down on a blanket and took a sunbath although we had our regular clothes on. We had for lunch French bread, ham, cheese, oranges, bananas and a bottle of wine.

Did I tell you my latest pictures are very good? I get a big thrill every time I look at them. I got a little carried away with the guards in front of the Palace in Monaco. I think I took something like 6 or 8 slides! I'll have to watch myself about that.

I've been wanting to visit La Garde-Freinet. The twin sister city of Newark [Delaware]. I was telling one of my French friends about it. She was very surprised and said that her mother was born in La Garde-Freinet! Some Saturday we are going together to visit.

Yes, I still see Georges. He's part of my group of friends. He often walks me home at night. I know he likes me, but I don't know how much. We don't date anymore. Sometimes we go with the rest of the gang to a movie. It's probably for the best. If we had continued, he probably would have eventually talked of marriage and that would <u>never</u> work. I have too many plans for when I get home.

Love,
Barb

March 10

Dear Mother & Daddy,

Here is main street in my most favorite town in all the world! I hate to think of ever leaving it. If you could just be here too I would be completely happy!

Diana and I are definitely going to Italy now in her car. We will probably leave around March 22. Sat. I'm going on an excursion to Arles. Saturday night I may go to a ball, "La Nuit des Lettres" – night of the Faculty of Letters.

Will write a letter after the weekend activities. I'm looking forward to receiving some stockings for my birthday.

Love, Barb

March 13

Dear Mother & Daddy –

I have spent a rather busy day and I'm now in the library. I will have to give a talk in the seminar course after Easter so I've been outlining my thesis - the Educational Theories of Fénelon! I would prefer to talk about the slides I will bring back from Italy, but it's good to have something in case that doesn't work out.

This morning I polished shoes, washed clothes, ironed 5 blouses and made a lunch. I had an orange and banana salad, hot chocolate, cheese, and cookies. Yesterday I bought some flowers - every now and then I [break] down and buy some. This time I have a beautiful bouquet of 5 large yellow tulips and six blue iris. They just remind me of Easter and colored eggs!! I don't eat at home too often because even that little snack was more expensive than a meal at the student restaurant.

The excursion to Arles Saturday was very interesting. We saw the remains of a Roman arena which is much like the Coliseum. We saw a Roman theater which was very much influenced by the Greeks - also churches and museums. Provence is very rich with Roman relics and ruins. I had always heard this, but I could not quite believe it until I saw for myself. The arena especially is a magnificent sight. They have bullfights in it and also plays and concerts from time to time.

We had a delightful lunch. I ate with Rick[43], the new Fulbright student, a very good English friend (unfortunately he has a French girlfriend), two other English people, two Swedes, and a boy from Switzerland. We had a marvelous time together. I'm now firmly convinced in what I believe already - people are nice the world over. You just have to know the right ones. For the most part the ideas and language that one has are the result of where he lives. Of course, this doesn't make me any less happier to be an American.

My teacher told me on the way that the huge rough stones in the fields brought back terrible memories. It seems the Germans forced French people to carry the stones into the field to prevent the Americans from landing.

We also went to an old medieval town built on the top of a hill called Les Baux. Only the ruins are left. This is the city from which bauxite got its name. Since the *Institut pour Étrangers* is

---

43 Presumably Richard Boulanger from Massachusetts (1929-1993).

paying half the cost for the excursions, we can go rather cheaply. The teacher also plans to take us to Avignon, Nîmes, and the *Pont du Gard*.

The dance was delightful. I borrowed a dress from Diana. It is a black satin sheath with black embroidery. It is now too small for her, and I looked fairly good in it, I think. We went in a group - my French girlfriends, Emily and I. All the boys in our group went home. Nevertheless, Rick came with some recruits and we kept adding to our party. It is much more in fashion to go to a dance in a group here than at home - in the States. I really enjoyed myself. I didn't get there until 11:30 and left at 4:00. The dance ended around 5:00. Some hours, eh!

Rick is a very nice man. I say man because he is 32 and has been married. Still he is lots of fun. I enjoyed dancing more with him than the others because we are so casual. We made up some of our steps, but we looked rather good anyway. He probably will go with us to Italy. I hope so because it would be nice to have a responsible man in the group. Did I tell you? We will probably leave March 22 or 23.

Sunday Emily and I were invited to dinner at Marseille. The man is the president of some organization promoting goodwill between the US and France. He was very warmly received when he toured the US and now he is trying to return the favor by inviting the Fulbrights to his home. We had a lovely meal with him, his wife, daughter, a girlfriend of the daughter's. After dinner, he took us for a car ride around Marseille. We returned again to his home, and I had him explain all about the different styles of French furniture. He had pieces beginning from Louis XIII all the way up to Empire.

I am enclosing an amusing article about French movies[44]. Although it is written in a humorous tone, much of what he says is true.

Love, Barb

---

44 Art Buchwald, *Going to a Paris Movie*. Barbara highlighted the following: "But waiting inside to pounce on you is an usherette, dressed like a guard in a women's prison. Usherettes in French cinemas must be tipped and heaven help you if you try to take a seat unescorted."

March 19

Dear Mother & Daddy,

Well tomorrow we leave for another grand adventure - Italy; and in less than a month, I will be calling you up "collect." Doesn't time fly? Every now and then I get a sick feeling in my stomach when I realize how time is running out on me! I can't possibly see everything I've planned - the thought of leaving my friends is far from a happy one. Life is very hard sometimes. The things you enjoy most are often snatched away.

I took one of the bank drafts down to the bank Friday in case I need some extra money in Italy. We had no problems until I went to the cashier. They refused to give me US dollars. I pointed out that it was stated on the check, "U.S. dollars" and I was not about to except French francs. You know sometimes you can get as much as a 20% reduction if you pay in dollars or travelers checks. Well, we finally hit a compromise. I excepted American travelers checks.

We are very excited about leaving. We are going in Diana's car. Diana, Rick, Emily, I, and another friend for part of the way. We plan to spend some time on the Italian Riviera, four days in Florence, four days in Rome, and some time in the Naples area. I haven't heard from New Castle school yet and I'm afraid they will send me a letter while I'm away, but I can't just sit around and wait. We plan to come back April 12 or before that if the money runs out.

I received a card from the Evans and Margie and Dave. Also a lovely letter from Kathy. I really feel closer to Kathy than anyone else. We just seem to be made to same way. She sent me the clipping about Howard S.'s wedding in June. Needless to say, neither one of us is too brokenhearted!! Kathy said, "I wonder if that poor girl knows what she's getting into!" Also – "I wonder if he discussed the rhythm method with her like he did with you?" For her birthday, I sent Kathy a bar of Spanish soap and some lavender perfume. Oh! I also sent a box of different odds and ends to me, ha! Your change purse is in it, Mother. Daddy, you can have any of the match covers which are duplicated. Sorry I couldn't send your gift from Tangiers, but it is too big for that box. I haven't got back to Marseille to find out about the trunk. I will do so right after vacation.

Rick is writing a doctor's thesis on Julian Greene - an American of French parents who wrote all his books in French. At any rate, this Julian Greene made a statement that the Shenandoah Valley is for him one of the most beautiful spots in the world. Not bad, eh!

I have a French friend who is writing a thesis and needs an American book very badly. The American publishers either didn't want to send just one book, or they said it would take at least three months for him to get. At any rate I think we could help Henri. Would you please go to a good bookstore and either buy the book or order it? Then send it to his address. He will reimburse me for all the expense. I would appreciate your help. Here is the necessary information:

Title: *Bernanos, his political thought and prophecy*
Author: Molnar, Thomas (I'm not sure which is his first name)
Publisher: Sheed and Ward, 1960, New York

Henri's address:

Villa "Malgrétout"
Berre-les-Alpes
(Alpes Maritimes)
France

Bernanos was a French Catholic writer.

Thursday night I went to see an excellent production of Racine's play *Andromaque*. I've read this play several times and really do like it! The actors were all dressed up in classical garb with a classical stage setting.

I have finally decided to shorten some of my skirts. I've been wearing the waistband turned down; but now that it's spring, I can wear more blouses and the waistband doesn't look so great!

Emily bought a record player so now I can buy some French records. I doubt that she will be very hard to get along with on the trip since there will be 4 of us.

It seems such a shame that I won't be hearing from you for 3 weeks, but then I'll have more mail when I get back. I have a rendezvous with Georges on my way through Nice, Monday - just to say "hello" and "good-bye."

Love,
Barb

Riviera dei Fiori - S. REMO
Palmizi sul Lungomare Imperatrice
Palmiers sur la promenade Imperatrice
Palm-trees on the Imperatrice sea-walk
Palmen auf der Seepromenade Imperatrice

March 21

Dear Mother & Dad,
 We arrived at San Remo last night. It is one of the most beautiful towns I've seen. It's filled with gorgeous flowers & flowing fountains. The gardens aren't nearly as formal as those in France!!
 The Italians are very friendly & cordial. Last night I ate Lasagna & drank red wine for dinner.
 We finally sent the Trucks to Bill & Mustafa — they were very good!
 I'm really looking forward to seeing Florence next. Love, Bob

Mr. & Mrs. W.R. Snow
504 Springhill Ave
Phillips Heights
Wilmington 3, Delaware
U.S.A.

Now I'm learning Italian ha! I have a book with French phrases converted into Italian ones.

March 21

Dear Mother & Dad,

We arrived at San Remo last night. It is one of the most beautiful towns I've seen. It is filled with gorgeous flowers and flowing fountains. The gardens aren't nearly as formal as those in France!

The Italians are very friendly and cordial. Last night I ate lasagna and drank red wine for dinner. We finally sent the 5 pictures to Bill and Mustafa. They were very good! I'm really looking forward to seeing Florence & Rome.

Love, Barb

Pisa - Piazza del Duomo

Dear Mother & Daddy, March

Well, I've always dreamed of
seeing the leaning tower of Pisa
and today I climbed it all the
way to the top!! I really feel
as though I've achieved one of
my major ambitions in life.
As you can see the three
buildings, the church, baptistry
and tower make quite an
impressive sight.

We met a delightful group of
young Canadian flyers last
night in the restaurant & we ate
in a delightful time. Love,

March 24

Dear Mother & Daddy,

Well, I've always dreamed of seeing the leaning tower of Pisa, and today I climbed it all the way to the top!! I really feel as though I've achieved one of my major ambitions in life.

As you can see the three buildings, the church, baptistry, and tower make quite an impressive site.

We met a delightful group of young Canadian[s] … last night in the restaurant, and they showed us a delightful time.

Love, Barb

Dear Mother & Daddy,

I think this is the best trip yet!! Italy is a delightful country, and the people so helpful & friendly. The Italian Riviera is more beautiful than the French, though I hate to admit it.

Florence is the world's center of culture, art, literature and beauty. This morning we went to High Mass at a lovely Florentine church called St. Maria Novella. I didn't get much out of the mass so I conducted my own services! The church is beautiful inside & out. I thought of you two & wondered if you would be in church. I would like so much to be in my own church with my family on Easter & Palm Sundays.

This afternoon I went to the Uffizi Galleries — an art gallery like the Louvre. Guess what? I have finally found out the painter of my picture of the Madonna. It is a copy from Andrea del Sarto's "La Madonna dei Arpie." This picture is very large & has more figures but I'm sure mine has been copied from it. I feel as though I made a discovery ha! ha!

Also this afternoon I went to a lovely concert in the Palazzo Vecchio (Old Palace) — they played music by Mozart, Bartok, and Debussy. Have met Bob Mortimer — a Fulbright at Toulouse & some friends from art. Hope you have a happy Easter & think of me. I will cash in on my share of the pickled eggs in August ki ki!

Love,
Ruth

Firenze
di
Buona Pasqua

Dear Mother & Daddy,

I think this is the best trip yet!! Italy is a delightful country, and the people so helpful and friendly. The Italian Riviera is more beautiful than the French, though I hate to admit it.

Florence is the world's center of culture, art, literature, and beauty. This morning we went to high mass at a lovely Florentine church called S. Maria Novella. I didn't get much out of the mass so I conducted my own service! The church is beautiful inside and out. I thought of you two and wondered if you would be in church. I would like so much to be in my own church and with my family on Easter and Palm Sundays.

This afternoon I went to the Uffizi Galleries - art gallery like the Louvre. Guess what? I have finally found the painter of my picture of the Madonna. It is a copy from Andrea del Sarto's *La Madonna delle Arpie.* This picture is very large and has more figures, but I'm sure mine has been copied from it. I feel as though I've made a discovery ha!

Also this afternoon I went to a lovely concert in the Palazzo Vecchio (Old Palace). They played music by Mozart, Bartok and Debussy. Have met

Bob - a Fulbright at Toulouse and some friends from Aix.

Hope you have a happy Easter and think of me. I will cash in on my share of the pickled eggs in August. Ha ha!

Love, Barb

THE CROPPED PICTURE OF THE *MADONNA OF THE HARPIES*.

are you the map?

TTA DI S. GIMIGNANO
Panorama · General view · Panorama

March 28

Dear Mother & Dad,
  We were all very sorry to leave Florence this morning, but time marches on!
  We visited an old medieval town above Florence called Fiesole this morning. Now we are passing thru this fascinating town on our way to Siena. We expect to reach Rome sometime Thursday.
  The scenery is beautiful but I miss the Riviera.
        Love,
          Barby

Mr. & Mrs. W. C. Snow
504 Springhill ave.
Phillips Hts.
Wilmington 3, Delaware
          U. S. A.

Are you following my trip on the map?

March 28

Dear Mother & Dad,

  We were all very sorry to leave Florence this morning, but time marches on! We visited an old medieval town above Florence called Fiesole this morning. Now we are passing through this fascinating town on our way to Siena. We expect to reach Rome sometime Thursday. The scenery is beautiful, but I miss the Riviera.

Love, Barby

Roma - Il Tevere di notte con la Basilica di S. Pietro

March 31

Tomorrow I plan to visit Saint Peters.
I am looking forward to my phone call on the 15th!!!!!

Dear Mother & Dad,

We have arrived at Rome! It is a beautiful city. Today I saw the famous Trevi Fountain (of *3 coins in the fountain* fame), Pantheon, Colosseum, Baths of Caracalla, etc.

We had a very unfortunate incident happen in that a professional robber stole Diana's purse - thus we spent the rest of the afternoon in the police station. In order to forget the unhappy experience and avoid the crowds, we are going on to Naples and will return Tuesday. I will write more in a letter when I return. I was quite impressed with Assisi. Love, Barb

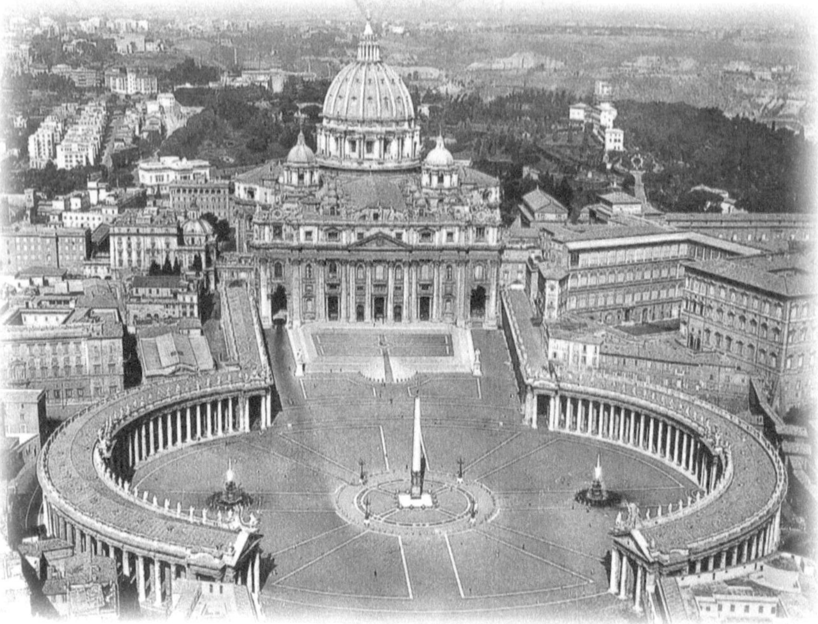

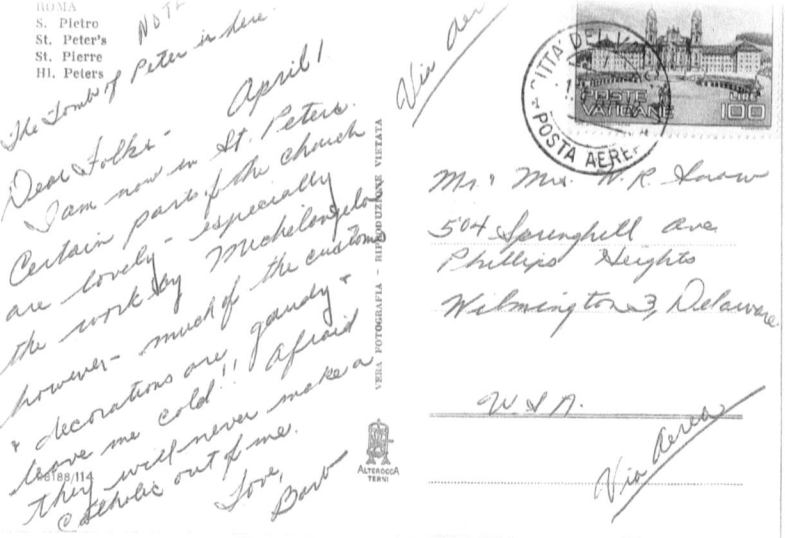

ROMA
S. Pietro
St. Peter's
St. Pierre
Hl. Peters

NOTA
The Tomb of Peter is here.

April 1

Dear Folks -
I am now in St. Peters.
Certain parts of the church
are lovely - especially
the work by Michelangelo
however - much of the customs
& decorations are gaudy &
leave me cold!! Afraid
they will never make a
Catholic out of me.
Love,
Barb

VERA FOTOGRAFIA - RIPRODUZIONE VIETATA
8188/114
ALTEROCCA TERNI

Via Aerea

CITTA' DEL ... POSTA AEREA
POSTE VATICANE LIRE 100

Mr. & Mrs. W. R. [illegible]
504 Springhill Ave
Phillips Heights
Wilmington 3, Delaware

U.S.A.

Via Aerea

April 1

The tomb of Saint Peter is here!

Dear Folks-

I am now in St. Peters. Certain parts of the church are lovely - especially the work by Michelangelo. However, much of the customs and decorations are gaudy and leave me cold! Afraid they will never make a Catholic out of me.

Love, Barb

CAPRI
Grotta Azzurra
Blue Grotto
Grotte d'azur
Blaue Grotte

Dear Mother & Daddy,
What a delightful Easter week-end!! Last night we saw the moon come up over Vesuvius on our way to Sorrento, near Naples.
Now I am in Capri & have just seen the Blue Grotto!!! The weather is beautiful. I sure wish you both were here with me.
Love, Bart

Mr. & Mrs. W. R. Snow
504 Springhill Ave.
Phillips Heights

Wilmington 3, Delaware
U.S.A.

April 2

Dear Mother & Daddy,

What a delightful Easter weekend!! Last night we saw the moon come up over Vesuvius on our way to Sorrento, near Naples. Now I am in Capri and have just seen the Blue Grotto!! The weather is beautiful. Sure wish you both were here with me.

Love, Barb

Tonight we stopped at a motel restaurant, and all of us realized how much we missed the U.S.

April 3

Dear Mother & Daddy,

Today we rode along the famous Amalfi Drive from Sorrento to Salerno. We stopped to see a lovely cove and also for lunch.

Then we came back by way of Pompeii which is marvelous. The town is still intact (the ruins that is). It is very charming & one can see Vesuvius in the distance. Tomorrow we go back to Rome for 2 days & then home. Love, Barb

April 6

Dear Folks,

We are now back in Florence on our way home to Aix - plan to reach Aix Sat. or early Sun. morning.

You will never guess - yesterday morning I attended an audience with the Pope!! I really found it disgusting! However, I made up for it by visiting the catacombs which I found very interesting and impressive.

The Pope blessed us and any religious articles we were carrying. I bought a cross for me and two medals. If Art Reed's wife would like a little medal of the Pope, I will be glad to send it.

Love, Barb

April 9

Dear Mother & Daddy,

I have made it back home safe and sound after a delightful trip. The weather was fine ... it didn't rain at all. All kinds of mail was waiting for me, so it was a recompense for not having any for almost 3 weeks.

Glady wrote me two letters and a card. The card was from Natural Bridge, Virginia. Her father is going to work someplace down south for 5 months. She said she thought of me when they passed through Staunton!! She's busy with school, chores, and is still taking graduate courses at Penn. I certainly do admire her ambition and stamina. Two of her students wrote me asking for information on France... It was really a cute letter!

Aunt Esther wrote a nice letter informing me that Danny's going to marry this summer - a Catholic. She is 5'7", slim, quiet, and very lovely according to Aunt Esther. She sent me a photo of her and Steven in her living room. It is quite modern with a large picture window almost reaching the floor. [Cousin] Linda is going to have a baby, in December I think. Aunt Esther was quite amused at thinking of Aunt Henry[45] as a grandmother!! Ha!

I am so glad you both are having fun traveling, bowling, clubbing, etc. Sometimes I have a guilty conscience when I think of all the wonderful things I'm doing and seeing and you can't be with me. I surely would have liked to be there when you visited Marvin and Virginia.

Daddy, I'm afraid I gave you the wrong impression when I write you about Aix. I do really love it, and it is the loveliest city I've ever lived in, but I don't mean I prefer France to the US. I was mainly comparing Aix to Wilmington. I like France and hope to return, but it can never compare to the US.

This is one thing I particularly liked about Italy. The Italians are quite friendly and very cordial to Americans. You were always proud to tell your nationality while in France sometimes you would prefer to conceal it.

So Delaware is going to participate in the Civil War again, eh! I think the whole idea is a bit silly and a waste of good money, but I would really like to see the reenactment of the Battle of Gettysburg. Maybe we could go with the Crawfords[46].

....

45 Lula Henryetta Heltzel Lambert (1918-2013).

46 Leonard (1914-1995) and Evelyn (1915-2000) Crawford. Leonard Crawford was a coworker of Barbara's father at the DuPont Company.

I'm so sorry I didn't get your letter about the hand towels in time!! However, I will send some from here as a Mother's Day gift. I also plan to visit Switzerland and England before I come home so I will pick some up there. Rick is going back to Florence next year, and I'm sure he would send us some from Italy. Florence is our favorite city in Italy. I've kept the address of a good hotel and restaurant for my next trip, whenever that may be!! I have already bought your birthday present, Mother, and Father's Day gift, Daddy.

I hear that Nancy and Eleanor are planning to tour Europe this summer. Why don't you call Eleanor and ask if she will be in London anytime during July? Maybe we can have a little rendez-vous! Kathy wrote saying she might visit the Scandinavian countries this summer.

I have not yet bought a summer skirt. Mainly because I haven't found one I like. I will now look around and ask. This trip was much better than the one to Spain because we stayed at nicer places. At least this time we had hot water. The problem was trying to find something to suit Rick and still not be too expensive.

I bought two pairs of shoes in Florence. The leather is so good; therefore I bought one pair of brown shoes for dress - my others are so out of style - and another pair for sport and teaching!

Now welcome to the big problem of the day! I still haven't heard from New Castle so I may be working in the 5 & 10 next year. I may write to some other schools in Delaware needing French teachers such as Stanton, Bridgeville, and Seaford, but I would really prefer New Castle. My future plans are to work a year, and then go to graduate school, then maybe to California. Rick is constantly raving about Santiago [San Diego?]; he says it's much like the Riviera of France.

Thanks so much for ordering the book for Henri. He will surely appreciate it! Your talk with Al must have been done him good. I had 6 letters from him when I returned yesterday evening. He has received a $2800 scholarship from Yale next year. Now I am convinced that he is brilliant.

Will write next time about my trip. Will call Saturday around 8 AM your time. I have heard from Roberta too. She is fine and seems more relaxed.

Love, Barbie

April 15 [Barbara's birthday]

Dear Mother & Daddy,

A large base of beautiful pink hydrangeas was waiting for me when I returned a few minutes ago! Thank you so much.

I have had a lovely day, as I usually do on my birthday. I guess I should be thankful that I'm so lucky in that respect. This morning as I was getting ready for cooking class, Jean Kinnon, my girlfriend from England, popped in with five beautiful long stem yellow roses and some *calissons* (little cookies - a specialty of Aix).

The cooking class was great fun. We prepared artichokes with a delicious sauce, lamb with a meat dressing and wrapped up in a sheet of flaky pastry, and brioches with jelly. Diana gave me a darling contemporary card.

The main highlight of the day was when I met Georges at the bus stop. He was going home to Nice, and I was to see him off as I often do. He handed me some pamphlets of Aix which he was keeping for me, but inside was this record that I wanted for months. It's the *Petit Prince*, by St.-Expéry narrated by Gérard Philipe - the movie idol of France who recently died. I saw him play one of his greatest rolls in *El Cid* in New York. The *Petit Prince* is a fairy tale which interests people of all ages. Georges didn't say much. He was rather embarrassed and just grinned. He's the main reason why I would like to come home as soon as possible. I am absolutely positive that we both love each other very much, but there's just no hope for us to get together. Don't worry, he is a lovely person and would never take advantage of me. I just can't stand the thought of never seeing him again. I keep telling myself it's better to have loved someone and enjoyed life for a while than to have never loved at all - but it all seems so tragic.

The other main highlight of the day was my call home. I'm so sorry you weren't home Daddy. The post office closes at 4 PM our time on Saturday. The call went through in about five minutes. Everyone was so nice and friendly. Emily gave me a box of candy. I really am fortunate to have such wonderful friends.

I definitely do not want the job at New Castle. As I wrote you before, I want very much to go to graduate school, and I must keep working on my French. If I can't find a teaching position, it would be better to work in a store and study French at night rather than teach English. I've written 7 other schools (5 in Del. and 2 in Long Island) so I might hear something yet.

The American Express division in Marseille says I can send my trunk straight through to Wilmington. I just hope it doesn't cost too much. I need to know the measurements of the trunk. Of course, they will all have to be converted into meters.

I would like to know my final cumulative index in case some of these schools ask me for it. It is something over 3.5, but I can't remember what.

Last night Emily and I had great fun popping popcorn on our hot plate. When we ate it, I remarked that I felt I should be watching a movie or TV.

I was very distressed to hear that Lois (my roommate in Paris and friend from Grenoble) has gone home. She was sick and had something like a nervous breakdown and finally decided to go home! I found this out in Rome from other Fulbrighters and have written to Cathie for more details. I surely hope she is all right now.

We Fulbrighters surely do get around! I met some in Florence and some in Rome. During the Mardi Gras, we met at Nice. One of the best books you can use is this *Europe on $5 a day*. That's why we are always running into each other.

I saw *The Misfits* the other night and was rather disappointed. Of course, the voices were dubbed and Gable just isn't himself without his voice. I never realized how important his voice is to his personality. Also, he is definitely an American type and doesn't sound too great spouting French; however, I thought even the plot was a little dull and stupid.

I read a good article in *Look* magazine about the effort to stomp out prejudices in our churches - that is so true. I think the church has made me more prejudiced than any other institution and Presbyterians are one of the most liberal-minded sects!

Rick Boulouger's mother sends him fudge & it arrives in good condition!!!!!!!!!!!!!!!!

Lots of love,
Barb

The Evans sent me 2 wedding pictures as a birthday present. Margie was really lovely...

April 20

Dear Mother & Daddy –

You can imagine my astonishment when I read that Daddy was in the hospital! I'm certainly glad you're coming along fine, Daddy. If I'd known, I would've sent you flowers. Who brought the ice cream? - the Crawfords?

Today I received a special delivery letter from Bridgeville, Delaware. They sent me a contract -all I have to do is sign and send in some forms. It sounds delightful. I can teach French I, II and III and next year French IV. The only drawback is the salary - $3900 or 4200 if the bill goes through that's in the Legislature. Also I don't even know exactly where Bridgeville is! I've always thought of southern Delaware as the country sister of Wilmington. I think I might wait a few days to see if I hear from any of the other schools - yet it does sound like a lovely opportunity to teach French - good experience for graduate school.

Now I must tell you about my audience with the Pope!![47] Also, you still haven't said if Art Reed's wife would like the medal I have that was blessed. Diana and I started out together. We bought some objects to have blessed. This is quite a racket - the avenue leading to St. Peter's is lined with souvenir shops for such occasions. We stood in a long line. Finally when the signal was given, everyone started running wildly – a priest almost knocked me down! Of course my card was the color which was the most far away. Finally I found myself in St. Peter's! Diana had disappeared, but we found each other later. There were no choirs – people were pushing and shoving until my feet were killing me. I almost decided to leave, but I doubt I could have gotten through the crowd.

Finally around 11:00 the Pope came. He was <u>carried</u> in in a big red chair. I heard waves of applause as he came near. Then he was paraded all around so we could get a look at him. He seems to have a very kind face and is one of the most favorite of the Popes. He gave his message in Italian and French; then it was translated into English, German, Spanish, etc. I am sure I did not receive such a wonderful experience with the proper respect. I was almost disgusted. Still I may

....

47 Pope John XXIII was pope from 1958-1963.

have acted like the others if it had been Kennedy!! Also as one of my friends pointed out, the Pope represents Jesus so in that light you can understand it better.

Yes, Diana's passport and all the car insurance papers were in her purse. She had to buy a new passport at the American Embassy for $10. We loaned her money until the American Express issued her new travelers checks.

Roberta sent me two birthday cards - her mother sent one. I wish I knew when Mrs. Stephenson's birthday was. Roberta also sent me a charm - a little ocean liner. When I get home, I will have to have two bracelets!- but the charms make such lovely souvenirs.

Rick has been invited to a wedding in Switzerland in June and he says he will take me as his guest. I hope everything works out so I can go. There's going to be a cocktail party before the wedding - a dinner afterward - and dancing still later.

Saturday I'm going on an excursion to Nîmes and the Pont du Gard. Nîmes is where the Maison Carrée is. Thomas Jefferson designed the University of Virginia after it and the Pont du Gard is one of the few Roman aqueducts still in existence and in _use_.

I've been following the news about Cuba with much anxiety. It's such a shame people like the Russians have to live in the same world as us. You probably have read by now that there is much speculation as to whether Gagarin actually rode around the earth in a satellite.

One of the things I enjoyed most in Rome was the catacombs. Also the Trevi fountain. We had a hotel right opposite it. I heard water each night before I went to sleep. My next big vacation will be spent in England, I think and then maybe I shall decide to tour the USA!! - Always must save the best for last.

Love, Barb

BARBARA IN FRONT OF THE TREVI FOUNTAIN

518 LE PONT DU GARD (Gard) — Aqueduc
main (Agrippa, gendre de l'Empereur Auguste
chargé de la direction des travaux)
19 avant Jésus-Christ

Dear Folks,

The excursion Saturday
was delightful! We had
picnic by the Pont du Gard
then walked over it
(the top). After lunch
went on to Nîmes +
saw the Roman arena +
the Maison Carrée. Hope
are coming along fine, Dad.

Mr. & Mrs. W. L. Snow
504 Springhill Ave.
Phillips Heights
Wilmington 3, Delaware
U.S.A.

PAR AVION

I have heard from 3 schools – but can't decide. The salaries down state are poor.

April 24

Dear Folks,

The excursion Saturday was delightful! We had a picnic by the Pont du Gard and then walked over it (on the top). After lunch we went to Nîmes and saw the Roman arena & the Maison Carrée. Hope you are coming along fine, Dad.

Love, Barb

Pont du Gard

Excuse pen - it's the cheapest I could find - a little less than 5¢ - it shows it, doesn't it? When are you going to write about your operation, Daddy?

Are you going to send me some <u>fudge</u> or food <u>soon</u>?

April 27, 1961

Dear Folks,

Guess you have been interested in the French problems recently![48] Things were fairly calm here - it was in Paris that everything was so exciting - especially the thought of paratroopers descending! The French officials waited for them three nights, but fortunately they never came. Most of the French really backed de Gaulle. Monday afternoon from 5 to 6 all the students and many of the townspeople went on strike to protest the rebellion and to support de Gaulle. In Aix, they marched down the streets singing *La Marseillaise* and shouting "down with fascism." I think maybe now that de Gaulle sees his strength, he

---

48 The Algiers putsch of 1961.

will quicken the negotiations and get this Algerian affair settled. Practically everyone is ready to accept the independence of Algeria except those Frenchmen living there.

Henri was delighted with your letter and wants me to express his appreciation since his English is a bit weak. I received your package last weekend. The stockings and girdle were most welcomed. Thank you so much.

Last Sunday night some of the kids (American) got up a party at Randy's - she has rented a little house out in the country - a delightful place for parties. I didn't feel much like going. Then Diana said, "But what are we going to do with the 23 candles if you don't come?" Thus, I decided since it was an excuse to give me a birthday party, I had better go. We drank wine and ate popcorn.

Mr. Watson, from the Fulbright Commission, came down to Aix Tuesday and Wednesday. He came with Rick to the student restaurant, but since there was such a long line he invited Rick and me to eat with him uptown. He is a delightful person and we had lots of fun. Rick had told him that I was one of the few Fulbright students who had such a good rapport with the students - <u>French</u>. Mr. Watson was quite pleased and asked me how I did it?

Mr. Watson was the one who took Lois home - to the US after her nervous breakdown. I am quite concerned about her. Cathie is supposed to come down from Grenoble this weekend so I'm hoping she will tell me all about it. It must've happened very quickly because when we were there in February, everything was fine.

I am still trying to decide about a job. I have not heard from anyone this week probably because of the stopping of airplanes in Paris. If I can get a job in Newark or Long Island, I will take it. Newark offers around $4,500 dollars compared to Bridgeville's $3,900. I wish I could just call them up - Newark sent me an application form. Also heard from Seaford - it's for $3,900 dollars and 7th and 8th graders. I'm sure I would lose my mind there! I still think it would be nice to get a job with DuPont so I could study nights.

Glady's children sent me a letter asking for information. I no sooner shipped them off a package than I got 24 letters from Roberta's class! They are very cute but stupid! When I showed my French friends one of their letters asking what kind of clothes do the French wear - Jacques said "Well, what do they think we wear?"

Georges brought back his motor scooter from Nice so when we are not fighting - he brings me home on the back.

Love, Barb

[Included with the letter is a newspaper clipping from Art Buchwald entitled *Four Sleepless Nights* chronicling the events of April 23-25.]

May 4

Dear Folks,

So glad to hear from your letters that Daddy is coming along fine. Your last letter was especially amusing, Daddy. I suppose it is necessary to "suffer", but I hope you can do as little of it as possible.

I'm still having a time deciding about teaching. I received a lovely letter from the principal at Stanton Junior High School. He said Ms. Stewart[49] and Janie spoke very highly of me. There are two positions open. One is all French except for one class in English. The other is half & half. He thinks I would be very good for teaching conversational French, which I think I would really enjoy after this year in France. The salary is $4400! I much prefer the location of Stanton to Bridgeville so I told him if offered a contract for the first position, I would accept it. Unfortunately, all this writing takes time, and I'm sure Bridgeville wants to hear

....

49 Margaret Stewart, French teacher at Alexis I. Dupont High School under whom Barbara did her student teaching.

from me. Maybe next week, you could call him - Mr. Robert Stradling-principal-Stanton J.H.S – 1800 Limestone Road – Stanton, Wilmington 4. If he is <u>definitely</u> sending me a contract, you could then call Mr. Flint in Bridgeville and tell him "no" for me. If this is too much trouble, don't bother. They will just have to realize that all this takes time. I also heard from Seaford – only $3900 – also filled out an application for Newark; however, I didn't care much for the faculty when I substituted there my junior year.

Yesterday, I gave my little talk "en français" to the Fulbright seminar group. I showed my slides from Italy. It was the first time I have ever seen them projected! What a delight!! We will have to visit around all our friends that have projectors when I get home - Stephensons, Evans, etc. At any rate I'm glad that's over with!

Emily wants to visit Switzerland next weekend and since time is running out, I'm in agreement. There's no Fulbright seminar next week, so we won't miss much. Thursday next is also a holiday - the Ascension. Money is low so we will have to do it very economically. We will only take our sacks. We can picnic at lunch and eat a warm meal for dinner. I have so wanted to visit Switzerland that I feel I must go! Also Georges is hardly speaking to me, and I will welcome the change of scenery!!

I've been trying to find out more about the trunk and everyone is so indefinite! We may have to pay a little more with the American Express, but at least I feel fairly sure that the trunk will get to Wilmington that way. I really don't know what the cost will be - probably between $25 and $50. Unfortunately, I only have $150 left for July so if you could send some money for the trunk, it will be greatly appreciated! I shall go to Marseille at the end of May to fill out the papers.

Cathie Oliver and 3 other lovely girls from Grenoble were here last weekend. It was such a delight to see Cathie again! She is a good friend of Lois's, you know. We all went around together in Paris. She would like me to travel with her this summer until she goes home on July 14. As we both want to see England, I think something can be arranged. I surely hope so.

If you send candy, can you send it air mail, like the cookies or is that too expensive? If not, you can just wait, and I will cash in on all the good food I've missed when I get home!!! Now that Spring is here & July is approaching, of course I will miss my friends, but most of them won't be in Aix after one or two years anyway. Besides I'm sure I won't miss them as much as I miss you both.

Thanks for sending in the check to Phi Beta Kappa. I keep forgetting about my income tax check. You may keep it yourself if you like. How much was it? You might be able to use it toward paying the insurance on my car.

Life is getting back to normal in France except some people have accused the American CIA for encouraging the generals to revolt. I certainly do hope this is not true. We should be back in Aix around the 15th.

Love,
Barb

Dear Folks,

We have not made it to Switzerland yet! Carolyn forgot her passport so we stopped off at Grenoble - had a delightful visit with Cathie. Now we are at Aix-les-Bains which I must admit is as delightful as our Aix! It is on the edge of Lac Bourget, the largest lake in France. We took a boat ride across to this abbey this morning. The scenery is lovely. You can see snow-covered mountains in the distance. The monks here are very polite & friendly.

We hope to get to Geneva late Tuesday...

Mr. & Mrs. ...
Phillips Heights
Washington, Delaware
U.S.A.

PAR AVION

Glady is coming to Europe this summer!!

May 1

Dear Folks,

We have not made it to Switzerland yet! Emily forgot her passport so we stopped off at Grenoble - had a delightful visit with Cathie. Now we are at Aix-les-Bains, which I must admit is as delightful as our Aix! It is on the edge of the Lac Bourget, the largest lake in France. We took a boat ride across to the Abbey this morning. The scenery is lovely. You can see snow covered mountains in the distance. The monks here are very polite and friendly.

We hope to get to Geneva late Tuesday morning. Emily is making arrangements about her passport. Love, Barb

Switzerland

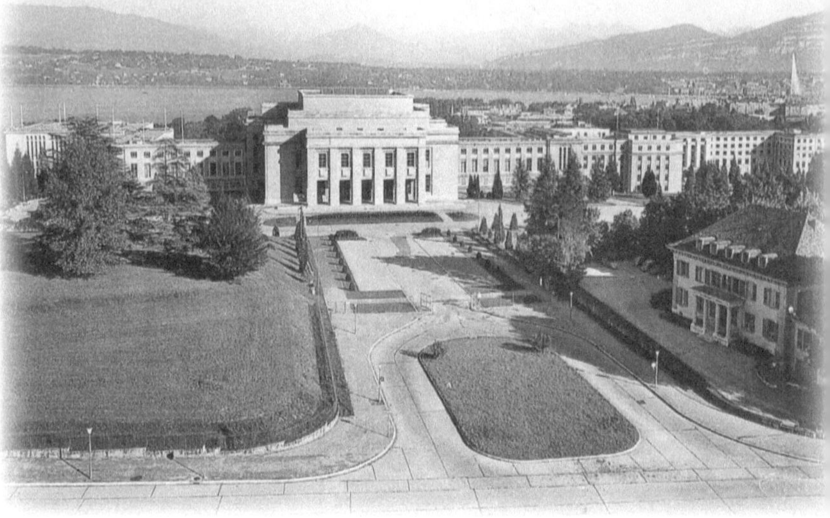

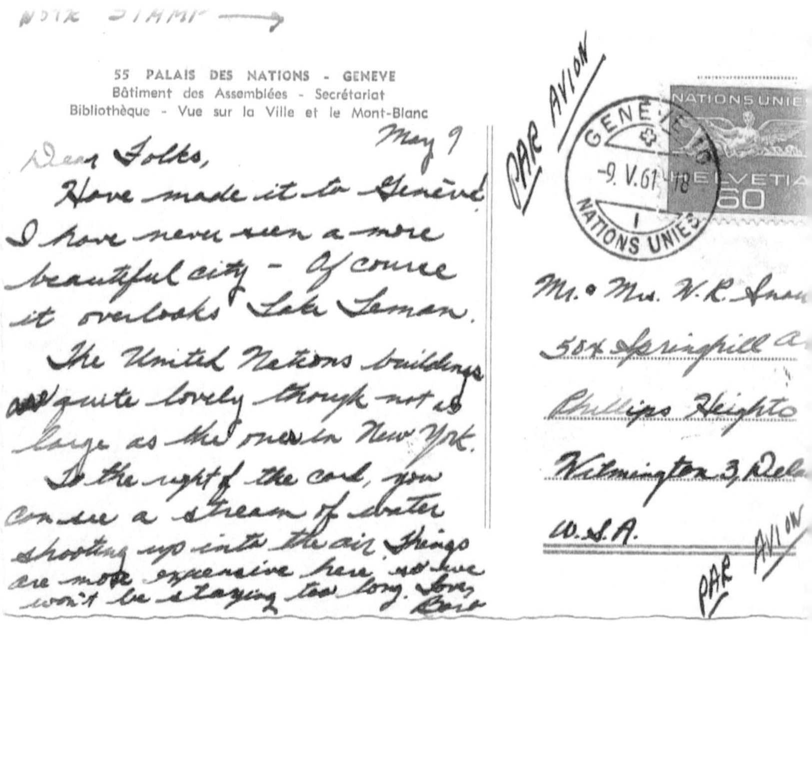

NOTE STAMP →

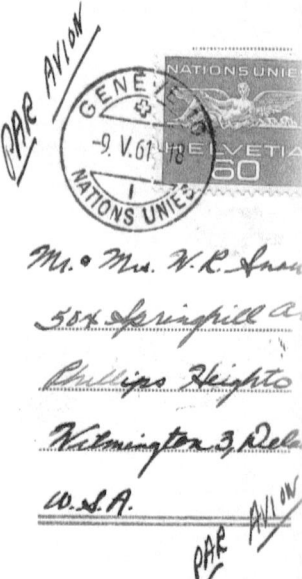

55 PALAIS DES NATIONS - GENEVE
Bâtiment des Assemblées - Secrétariat
Bibliothèque - Vue sur la Ville et le Mont-Blanc

May 9

Dear Folks,

Have made it to Genève! I have never seen a more beautiful city - Of course it overlooks Lake Leman.

The United Nations buildings are quite lovely though not as large as the ones in New York.

To the right of the card, you can see a stream of water shooting up into the air. Things are more expensive here so we won't be staying too long. Love, Bere

PAR AVION

GENÈVE 10 -9. V. 61 -18 NATIONS UNIES

NATIONS UNIES HELVETIA 60

Mr. & Mrs. W. R. Snow
58X Springhill A
Phillips Heights
Wilmington 3, Dela
U.S.A.

PAR AVION

May 9

Dear Folks,

Have made it to Geneva! I have never seen a more beautiful city - of course it overlooks Lake Léman.

The United Nations buildings are quite lovely though not as large as the ones in New York. To the right of the card, you can see a stream of water shooting up into the air. Things are more expensive here so we won't be staying too long. Love, Barb

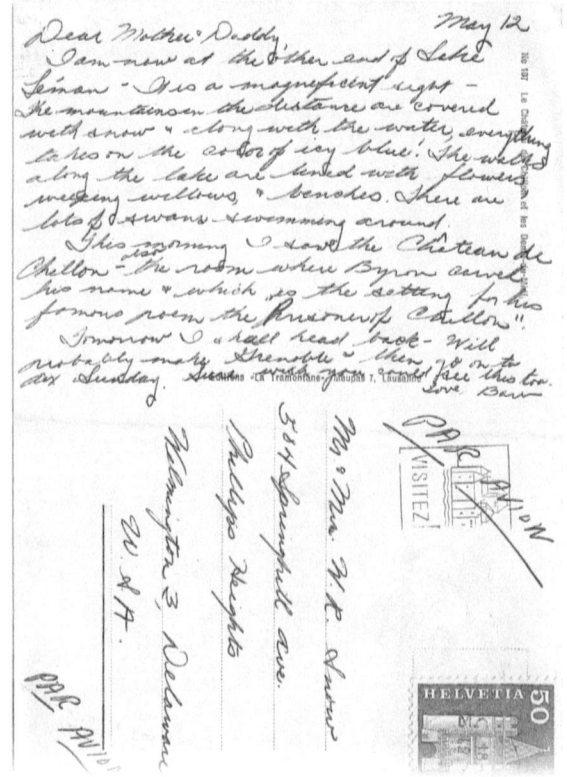

May 12

Dear Mother & Daddy,

I am now at the other end of Lake Léman. It is a magnificent sight. The mountains in the distance are covered with snow and along the water, everything takes on the color of icy blue! The walks along the lake are lined with flowers, weeping willows, and benches. There are lots of swans swimming around.

This morning I saw the Château de Chillon - also the room where Byron carved his name and which is the setting for his famous poem "The Prisoner of Chillon".

Tomorrow, I shall head back. Will probably make Grenoble & then go on to Aix Sunday. Sure wish you could see this too. Love, Barb

Thanks so much for the fudge. It is even better than the famous Swiss chocolate!!

May 17

Dear Mother & Daddy –

Sorry I haven't written sooner, but it seems like I have a million things to do before June 15. I arrived in Aix Sunday evening after a delightful trip. Monday I spent washing clothes, hair, & me - also wrote four letters to different schools - Stanton, Bridgeville, Newark, Seaford. A contract for $4500 dollars was waiting for me from Newark; however I'm not sorry I'm losing the extra $100 at Stanton. Newark sent me an application and then a contract, just form letters - nothing describing the school or the position I could have. They weren't nearly as cordial or enthusiastic as Stanton and Bridgeville. Mr. Stradling wrote saying Janie Lachno and Miss Stewart thought highly of me so that probably helped a lot!

Thank you so much for sending the postcard from Washington to Mustafa. He and Bill wrote thanking Emily and me for our cards from Italy (I had forgotten to send any) and also mentioned yours. They still want us to come back to Tangiers and I would really like to go! Mustapha's brother's wife had another baby - that makes eight now!!

I've been shortening summer clothes now. Everything turned out okay except the pleated Arnel sheath. It doesn't look very good at the bottom. I took it to a seamstress today, but she said she couldn't do any better so I will have to wear it the way it is. It packs the best of all my dresses.

Twice a year a Fulbright representative from each student group goes to Paris, and they discuss with the Commission our major problems. Rick went for us in Aix. He said that the major problem was finding friends.... Many of the Fulbrighters and other Americans have felt lonely and not wanted. Mr. Watson then proceeded to tell them about me and my French friends. Rick says I will go down in Fulbright history as the best goodwill ambassador - ha ha! I suppose I have been very fortunate; however I do not feel the same rapport with my French friends as I do with my best friends at home. I really am beginning to miss Glady, Kathie, Roberta, and you too. I suppose it will even be a little difficult when I get home since so many people my age are married and having children. I hope I can make some friends at Stanton so I won't feel like the fifth wheel! I really don't envy anyone ---- yet.

I'm afraid I lost my reputation of being a goodwill ambassador at the bank. I am really fed up with the stupidity and lack of efficiency of French officials. I tried to get my 3 other bank drafts cashed today. This time they wouldn't even give me the travelers checks. Since I've been living in France over 6 months I'm considered a French citizen and can have only francs. Well, by the time I finished, I'm sure they realized I didn't consider myself a French citizen and would rather die than become one!! I don't think I have ever been so furious! Now I am writing to the American Express at Nice. If they won't help me, I suppose I'll just have to take francs, but they have a very low exchange rate in Germany and England. If you can think of another solution, please let me know.

Dr. St. Aubyn wrote saying he is coming over for 2 months and hopes we can get together. He is coming to Aix for the music festival but I will have left. There may be a possibility of our meeting in Paris the week before I come home. Jackie Marvel, a very nice girl in French, got the Fulbright for next year. I hope I can talk to her before she leaves. I always thought she was the most responsible person in the French club.

My trip was lovely, especially after I lost Emily. I just can't stand her. Heaven knows, I've tried. She forgot her passport so we ended up in Aix-les-Bains waiting for it. Fortunately Aix-les-Bains is a lovely place. I didn't tell you before, but we had a little accident. We were walking alongside the road and a motorcycle knocked Emily down. It was dark and I was really frightened at first. I put my coat under her head and then she started talking. I didn't let her get up for awhile, but she only needed 2 stitches in her ankle. The people who stopped were lovely, and I asked someone to call an ambulance for the motorcyclist. He was groaning and bleeding. Then while Emily went back for her passport to Grenoble the next day, I had to explain everything to the police, who were also very nice.

We finally made Geneva Tuesday morning. I really enjoyed it, especially the UN and the Cathedral Saint Peter's where Calvin preached. Thursday we took a boat up the lake. Since I was running low on money, I couldn't go to both Lausanne and Montreux so I chose Montreux. Emily (whose fault it was that I didn't have my money because of her passport and accident) got off at Lausanne. The two days in Montreux where the most enjoyable of the whole trip; however, I'm very glad Cathie Oliver and I will be together this summer because I was afraid to do much at night by myself. At dinner one night, I met a lovely German girl and we agreed to meet again for dinner the next night. To be continued.

Love, Barb

May 26

The Fulbrighters are signing an organized petition for Pres. Kennedy when he comes asking the Fulbright program be continued. As of now, they only have enough money for 2 more years.

Dear Mother & Daddy,

    I was very happy to learn that you are taking a little vacation. I wish I could have come with you too. I would like very much to see the Virginia relatives before starting school in the fall - maybe something can be arranged.

    I am quite concerned how to pack my slides and *santons* - little figurines from Provence. I'm afraid something will happen to them in the trunk; and yet if I cart them around with me, they could also get broken or damaged. I have good news about the trunk. I can send it straight through from Marseille to Wilmington C.O.D. I hope you don't mind. It should cost somewhere around $25 or $30. We can't tell for sure until it has been weighed. I will repay you when I get my first paycheck. It should arrive in New York around July

23 and the American Express in New York will send it down. If it has not arrived by the time I do, we will have to check about it.

I received a lovely letter from Glady with an application form for her school several weeks ago. She said I could live with them in bad weather, or maybe we could rent an apartment. It was very thoughtful of her, but I still would rather be in Stanton. We will probably find times to get together, and I would like very much also to make some new friends.

I received an announcement of Danny's wedding which I thought was not at all necessary. If you would not like to include me in your present, they're not getting anything from me! When you are down to your last 5 NF and are anxiously awaiting the Fulbright check (it came today), you really can't appreciate this kind of thing, especially since I already knew about it from Esther. I sent her a card this week....

Yes, Cathie and I plan to visit some in Germany and England. I thought I had mentioned that. At any rate I shall enjoy her a great deal. There's a possibility that one of her friends will have a car. She is sailing home July 14 on *SS United States*. I have thought some about changing my reservation and coming home with her as I've had enough of traveling and I'm anxious to come home; but I really would like to have some slides of Paris and see some places I missed before.

Another Fulbrighter from Aix is sailing the same time as I am on the same ship, so I will still have someone around I know if I need company. Right now I think I've reached the stage where I enjoy being alone!! Doesn't sound like me, does it? An English friend is going to invite me to her home in Chester and show me around. If we go down to Liverpool, I will stop in to see Jean Kinnon's mother. One of the English boys gave me his phone number and said he would take me out to dinner. I have a feeling I'm going to like London and England after all. I've changed my ideas more about the English than the French.

Emily and I are inviting some of our French friends over for the 4th of June for cake and punch. We're not quite sure how it will work out yet, but we thought we would have them in the garden. Then I shall start packing my trunk and be off as soon as I get news from Cathie.

I must tell you about the bullfight at Nîmes in the Roman arena. We went at 12:00 to get seats -sat on concrete blocks and the fight started at 3:30!!

First there was a great procession with everyone participating coming out to salute the president of the fight. Then the bull charged out followed by the picadors. These are two men mounted on horses who stick the bull with wicked-looking sticks. The bull butts the poor horses who were dressed in padding, but often they fell down. The horses are blindfolded.

Part II - the banderilleros – these are men dressed in gay costumes who stick banderillos - pointed sticks decorated with crêpe paper into the bull's neck to weaken his shoulder muscles.

Part III - the matador dressed in a fancy costume, often gold, comes out with a red cape and sword and demands permission to kill the bull. After playing around a few minutes, he sticks the bull with his sword. The good bullfighter, Ordóñez[50], got his bull every time on the first try. Once he was awarded the two ears from the bull he had killed; however, the other two matadors were not so good. It took one six times and the whole affair was a butchery!! I much prefer the Provençale bullfight where the bull is not killed or hurt.

I made a slight mistake about the bank! They consider me a French resident not a French citizen.

Enclosed - medal for Mr. Reed's wife. It has been blessed by the Pope!!

Love,
Barb

---

50 Antonio Ordóñez Araujo (1932-1998).

June 2

Dear Mother & Daddy –

Thank you so much for the money! It was quite a relief. Crédit Lyonnais gave me $200 worth of travelers checks without batting an eye! Thank heavens for the American Express company. I finally sent my bank drafts to the American Express at Nice who in turn saw that I was issued $150 worth of travelers checks here in Aix. They, of course, charged a fee; but it was well worth it. I should be all right now as far as money is concerned and will try to bring some back with me.

Thanks also for the punch recipe. I had decided to make something like that, but had decided to use too much of everything, so now I have a better idea. There's no such thing as <u>frozen</u> orange juice in Aix! You are lucky when you find it in a can. I did, but the juices are all American products.

Diana, Emily, and I had lots of fun last week when we went to see the Gypsy festival[51].... We missed the procession, but we saw the church service - Catholic of course and extremely emo-

---

51 The Church of Les-Saintes-Maries-de-la-Mer is the site of pilgrimages.

tional. Candles were burning everywhere. It was a wonder the place didn't burn down. We were afraid to get too entangled with the mob so we watched from outside. Afterwards some of the French children of the town (Saintes-Maries-de-la-Mer) dressed up in darling little provençal costumes and danced. The whole trip was worth it just to see that.

Diana, Maryanne, and Jackson left yesterday morning. It was rather sad, but we are all planning to meet again back in the States. Jean Kinnon and I saw them off. The car was so loaded down, I thought it would have to crawl away! Diana and Jackson are going to Germany to the Goethe Institut where they will have intensive courses for two months!

Enclosed are two photos and some clippings I thought might interest you. The French are certainly being very gracious to our president. I'm very proud of him and his lovely wife. Some of the French kids said the other day that Jackie is prettier than Grace Kelly. I am in agreement when her hair is out of her face.

I have heard again from Cathie! I shall go up to Grenoble the 15th and then we will tour France in a car. By July 1, I shall go to England with or without them. As I have made plans to be there. I hope to get back to Paris around July 20 or 21st. After June 15 you could write me at the American Express - Paris and London.

Lots of love, Barb

June 9

Mother & Daddy,

Hope you had as much fun on your vacation as your cards sounded like you did! I just finished my trunk - I think! How everything got back in, I don't know. Most of my flat shoes have had it so I'm giving them to Madeleine, the maid - also two skirts and a dress. She said she would gladly take anything for her relatives. The transport co. is coming for it tomorrow and they'll take it into Marseille Monday. Tuesday I will go in with the key and inventory list. I've been busy sending packages - you should receive about nine - <u>especially</u> one for Daddy and my slides which I registered.

Our party was a big success! Thanks again for the punch recipe. Fortunately Mme Roman was not here and Madeleine was a big help. Emily bought two box cakes - one chocolate and one marble and baked them. I made the punch and floated strawberries in it. We had our friends in the garden and played Emily's record player. It was lots of fun, and I'm glad we did something for them. They've been so good to us.

You should see my new hairdo! I remarked to Jean that my hair needed cutting and so she recommended a place. They naturally fixed it like the French so my hair is now short but rather high on top - still with bangs. Everyone seems to like it, but it is going to be more difficult to set. I told Jean that I wish my mother could see me now - so she took a picture of me. I am quite pleased with the change myself.

Everyone here wears sandals so I broke down and bought a pair. I think they will be particularly nice this summer for touring. I also bought 2 cheap blouses at Monoprix[52] as most of my clothes are not very cool for summer; however, I'm also packing a wool skirt and sweater for the uncertain British weather.

Annette wrote me a lovely letter. She still wants me to visit her so I will be near Chester, England July 7, 8, and 9th. I've also met her parents - very lovely people - who came to visit her in Aix. After that, I shall go on to Stratford-on-Avon to see a play or two! I'm really getting excited. Jean is going to give me her brother's telephone number. He is a "Bobbie" in London[53].

---

52 A French retailer.

53 Ian H. Kinnon (1933-1993).

The other day I went to see M. Giniés to get some of the recipes I had missed. He invited Jean and me into his dining room and served us tea. He knew exactly which days I had missed. Before I left he gave me the address of his son in Paris - so if I have time, I may call on him. I also bought a French measuring cup to help with my cooking.

I received a card from Cathie. The plans are as follows: she and her friend Louise, who has a car, will pick me up here at Aix the afternoon of the 16th. Then we will go to Carcassonne, then on to the Basque country between Spain and France, then up to the Loire Valley to see the beautiful château. If they don't want to get to England by July 1, I may have to leave them.

I can't find any lens solution and it's too late for you to send me some here; however, if you would care to airmail me a bottle c/o American Express in London, I would appreciate it. Barnes & Hind wetting solution (pink). In the meantime, I suppose I'm left with no other alternative than using a French product. Also, please send letters there until July 15. Then you can send them c/o American Express, Rue Scribe, Paris 9. I'm looking forward to traveling this summer, but even more toward coming home.

Love,
Barb

P.S. Mme Roman is being as nasty as ever. Every day she thinks of ways to get more money out of us! First, Americans turn on the lights during the day time so we should pay more for electricity! Now also more for the record player. We've already paid the equivalent of $2.00 more to our rent. I'm about ready to tell her where to go. She's really going to have to work to get any more money out of us!!

Garden Party with Barbara
Seated on the Right

Compagnie des Gastronomes de Provence
du Comté de Nice et du Comtat Venaissin
FRANCE

COURS DE CUISINE PROVENÇALE
Organisés à l'usage des Etudiantes fréquentant l'Institut d'Etudes Françaises pour Etudiants Etrangers de la Faculté des Lettres d'Aix-en-Provence et l'Institute for American Universities

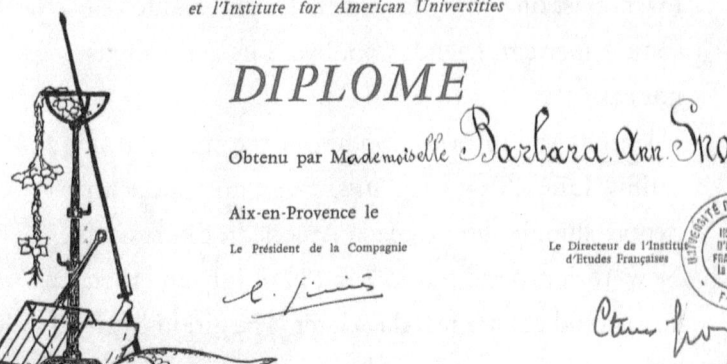

DIPLOME

Obtenu par Mademoiselle Barbara Ann Snoss

Aix-en-Provence le

Le Président de la Compagnie

Le Directeur de l'Institut d'Etudes Françaises

June 16

Dear Mother & Daddy –

Here I sit in the garden waiting for Cathie and Louise to arrive. I certainly hope they come soon as I feel rather sad. I ate dinner (lunch) with the kids; and they gave Emily and me each a record and autographed the cover. After dinner they all kissed me goodbye and I couldn't keep from crying. Then I went past one of my favorite cafés and had to tell some American friends goodbye. Life certainly is not easy!!

Here is the information about the trunk. It is sailing June 28 on the *Adventurer*, an American export ship. It should reach American Express in New York around the 15th or 18th of July and then you should get it a few days later. The girl in Marseille said it would cost about $30. This includes travel from Aix to Marseille, Marseille to New York, and insurance for $500 all the way. It does not include New York City to Wilmington. I must seem to be arriving home by bits. I hope all my packages make it, especially Daddy's Father's Day gift & a package of slides.[54]

....

54 Possibly a dagger from Morocco.

Thanks for the information about Dr. St. Aubyn. I hope this won't alter his plans. I have not heard from him again so I don't know if we will get together or not. I feel like organizing a movement to oust Perkins![55]

Here is the American Express address in London - Haymarket, London S.W. 1, England. You have Paris – 11 Rue Scribe, Paris (9).

I'm thrilled about Glady's coming to Europe and may be able to see her in London. If not, I shall certainly find her in Paris. It will be so exciting to see someone from home.

Annette sent me a lovely letter inviting me to her home near Chester so I will be there the 7th, 8th, and 9th of July. Jean Kinnon wants me to stay at her place in Liverpool one night even though she won't be there.

Yes, I took the pictures myself. I was angry with myself because I bought the wrong kind of film and got photos instead of dispositifs, but they did turn out very well. The girl at the camera store congratulated me on how good they were.

Aunt Ruby sent me a lovely letter and suggested that perhaps I could show my slides to her garden club!

....

55 President of the University of Delaware.

Emily left last week thank heavens! She is hitch-hiking with an American Fulbright boy - very nice guy. Can't see what he sees in her. At any rate while I was packing my one trunk she came back and packed 7 trunks or suitcases all at the same time. It was utter of chaos!! I had told her I wanted the room free to pack my trunk the few days before the men came to get it, but that made no difference! Everyone says I must have the patience of a saint to have put up with her all year.

Could you call Eleanor and tell her I won't be able to see her because her schedule is different from mine? She begins in London and ends with Paris while I will be there in the middle of her schedule. This will save me time and money if you call her.

Before Diana left she unloaded me with all the things she didn't want or couldn't use. One was a darling little oven you put on the top of a hot plate and a box of Betty Crocker date bar mix (her mother really kept her stocked with American products - one time she sent 19 cans of soup). Everyone thought it was a little silly. Anyway, Jean Kinnon came over and we tried the date bar mix. It was so good that I bought an American cake mix with chocolate icing. We tried this Wednesday and it also was a huge success. We ate the whole thing in one sitting in the garden. The weather has been delightful. I shall miss the garden and dogs.

I met a lovely elderly American couple the other day who raved about the château in the Loire Valley so I am glad I am going. Jean Kinnon showed me the English money one day and helped me count it. It is by far the most difficult. All the other countries I've been to are much like us.

I saw a good movie the other night, *Kapò*. It was all about life in a German concentration camp. I had no idea how terrible they were. This movie and the Eichmann trial are bringing me up-to-date. It just seems inconceivable and then when I see the German kids here, I can't connect them with their predecessors.

Write me soon - to London.

Love, Barb

Back To Paris

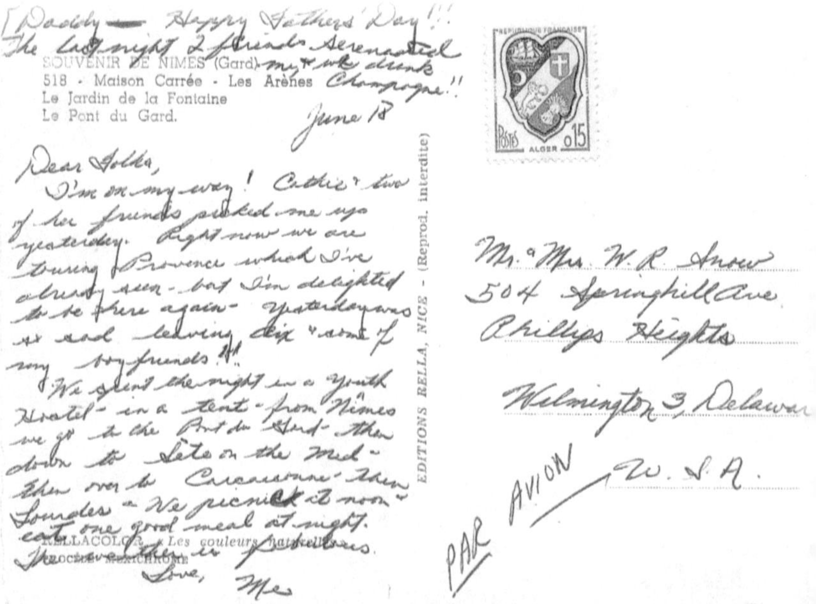

SOUVENIR DE NIMES (Gard)
518 - Maison Carrée - Les Arènes
Le Jardin de la Fontaine
Le Pont du Gard.

[Daddy — Happy Father's Day!!
The last night 2 friends serenaded
my + we drank Champagne!!
June 18

Dear Folks,
I'm on my way! Cathie + two
of her friends picked me up
yesterday. Right now we are
touring Provence which I've
already seen - but I'm delighted
to be here again - Yesterday we
we cool leaving six + seven of
my boy friends!!
We spent the night in a Youth
Hostel - in a tent - from Nîmes
we go to the Pont du Gard - then
down to Sète on the Med -
then over to Carcassonne - then
Lourdes - We picnic it at noon +
eat one good meal at night.
Love,
Me

Mr. + Mrs. W.R. Snow
504 Springhill Ave
Phillips Heights

Wilmington 3, Delaware
W. S. A.

PAR AVION

Daddy - Happy Father's Day!! The last night 2 friends serenaded me, and we drank champagne!

June 18

Dear Folks,

I'm on my way! Cathie and two of her friends picked me up yesterday. Right now we are touring Provence which I've already seen, but I'm delighted to be here again. Yesterday was so sad leaving Aix and some of my boyfriends!!

We spent the night in a youth hostel - in a tent - from Nîmes we go to the Pont du Gard then down to Sète on the Med - then over to Carcassonne - then Lourdes. We picnic at noon and eat one good meal at night. The weather is fabulous. Love, me

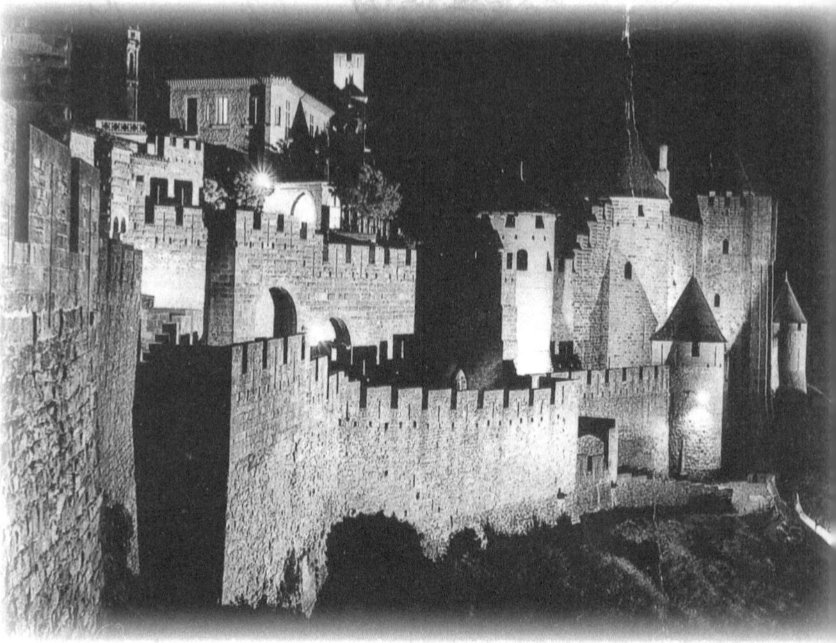

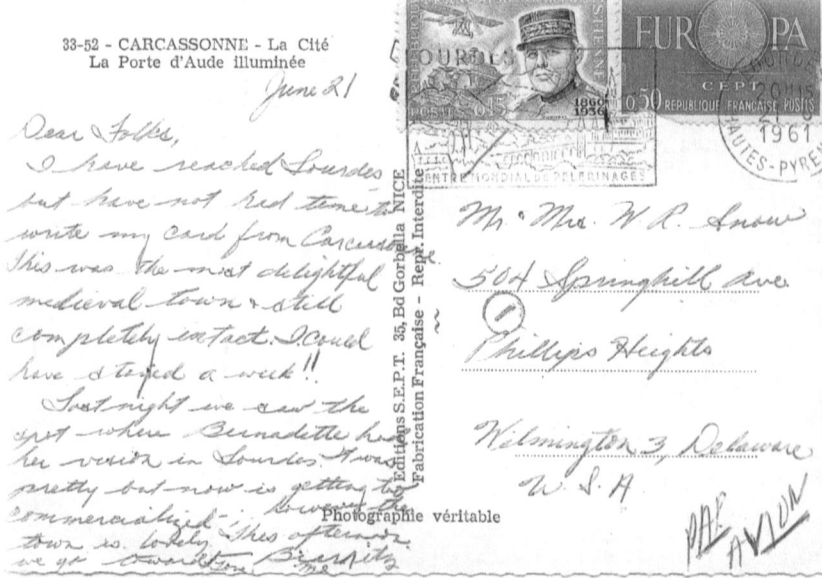

33-52 - CARCASSONNE - La Cité
La Porte d'Aude illuminée

June 21

Dear Folks,
I have reached Lourdes but have not had time to write my card from Carcassonne. This was the most delightful medieval town & still completely intact. I could have stayed a week!!
Last night we saw the spot where Bernadette had her vision in Lourdes. It was pretty but now is getting too commercialized - however the town is lovely. This afternoon we go toward Biarritz.

Mr. & Mrs. W. R. Snow
504 Springhill Ave.
Phillips Heights
Wilmington 3, Delaware
U.S.A.

PAR AVION

Editions S.E.P.T. 35, Bd Gorbella NICE
Fabrication Française - Repr. Interdite

Photographie véritable

June 21

Dear Folks,

I have reached Lourdes, but have not had time to write many cards from Carcassone. This was the most delightful medieval town & still completely intact. I could have stayed a week!

Last night we saw the spot where Bernadette had her vision in Lourdes. It was pretty but now is getting too commercialized - however the town is lovely. This afternoon we go toward Biarritz.

Love, Me

LOUISE AND BARBARA

Barbara and Cathie in front of the
Château de Chenonceaux

PARIS
372 - l'Arc de Triomphe illuminé

Dear Folks,
  A month from today I will
see you!! I can hardly
wait. I am ready now.
  We came to Paris saw Racine's
Britannicus at the Comédie
Française — (What luck)
Cathie & her friend went on to
Germany, but I am to meet
them July 10. Rick Boulanger
is here and we had a very (yesterday)
nice dinner + café afterwards.
  Tomorrow I leave for London
I leave Paris at 10:00 & will
arrive there at 6:30. At London I
am to meet Maryanne, a Fulbright
from Aix.   Love, Barb

Mr & Mrs W. R. Snow
304 Bunghill Ave.
Phillips Heights
Wilmington 3, Delaware
        U.S.A.

PAR AVION

Yesterday I saw the Rodin museum and his famous work "The Thinker"

June 30

Dear Folks,

A month from today I will see you!! I can hardly wait. I am ready now.

We came to Paris & saw Racine's <u>Britannicus</u> at the Comédie Française (what luck). Cathie and her friend went on to Germany, but I am to meet them July 10. Rick Boulanger is here so we had a very nice dinner & cafe afterwards.

Tomorrow I leave for London. I leave Paris at 10:00 and will arrive there at 6:30. At London I am to meet Marianne, a Fulbrighter from Aix.

Love, Barb

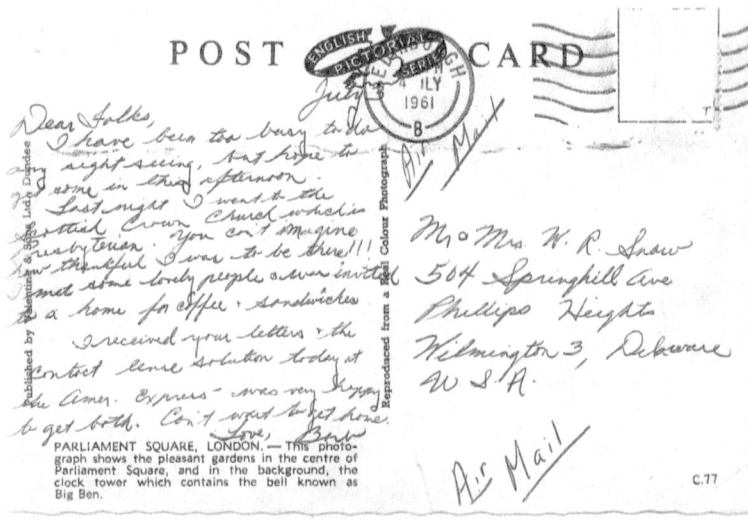

PARLIAMENT SQUARE, LONDON. — This photograph shows the pleasant gardens in the centre of Parliament Square, and in the background, the clock tower which contains the bell known as Big Ben.

July 3

Dear Folks,

I have been too busy to do any sightseeing, but hope to get some in this afternoon. Last night I went to the Scottish Crown Church which is Presbyterian. You can't imagine how thankful I was to be there!!! I met some lovely people and was invited to a home for coffee and sandwiches.

I received your letters and the contact lens solution today at the Amer. Express – was happy to get both. Can't wait to get home.

Love, Barb

July 4 [1961]

Dear Mother and Daddy,

Please forgive me if I have been tardy in writing, but I am having a hard time keeping to my schedule. I wrote you a card from London and then lost it. Maybe someone will find it and mail it to you.

The crossing was very calm except that I spent most of my time standing in line (to board the ship, get passport checked, fill out embarkation card, buy lunch, etc.) I'm hoping I will have enough money to fly back. The boat train into London was 2 hours late due to a signal failure. I met (by Providence I think) an Indian student from Kenya who had been a student in Paris. We had a terrible time getting taxi, but finally he took me to the place where he was staying. I meant 6 of his Indian friends who are the most charming and delightful young people you would want to know!! We had a snack together Saturday night and were together most of Sunday.

Meanwhile I was dying to get away to see London (even though I enjoyed them a great deal). I finally used church as an excuse - it was a wonderful experience - I went to the Church of Scotland which is Presbyterian and almost exactly the same as us. If I were to choose another country other than the US, I think it would be Scotland. The people at church were very friendly and one lady invited me to her home with the other church members for coffee and sandwiches. She made me think what mother might be like 20 years from now. She was spry, witty, and talkative!!

Monday, I was thrilled to get your letters and the contact lens solution. My friends took me to the Indian club for lunch and one girl found a place for me to stay when I go back. It is very hard to find anything inexpensive because London is now being overrun by American tourists - some of which are not good ambassadors.

Monday night I took a bus for Edinburgh. We arrived this morning at 10:20. I decided it would be rather unthoughtful for me to celebrate July 4 in Great Britain so I have done nothing except wonder what you were doing.

I love Edinburgh although it is chilly and I don't feel as much at home here as in Aix naturally. Tomorrow I take a trip to Loch Lomond and surrounding country.

This afternoon I attended (half by accident) the meeting of the Presbytery of Edinburgh and met an American doing a TV program on the uniting of Christianity who took me to dinner- to be continued. I saw John Knox's house.

Lots of love, Me

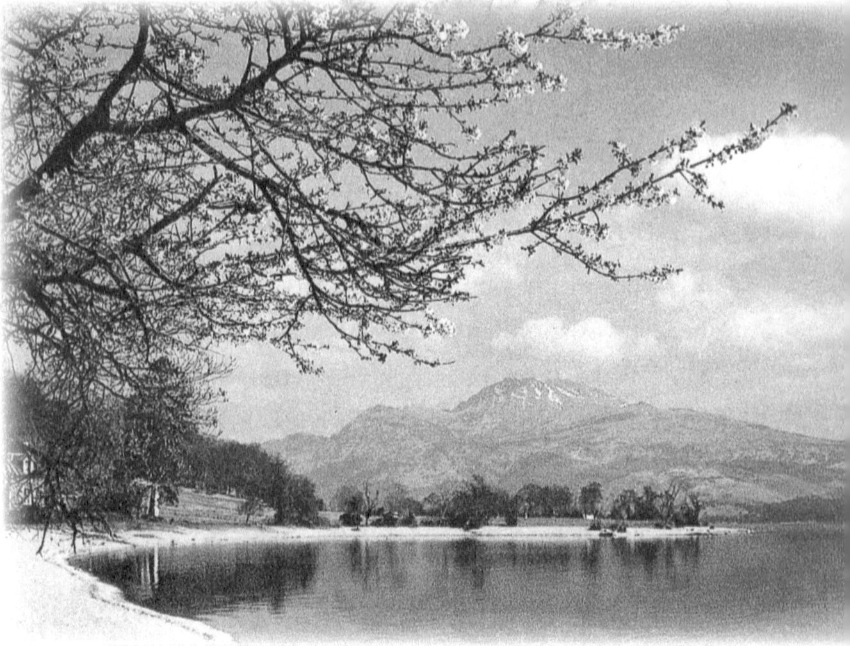

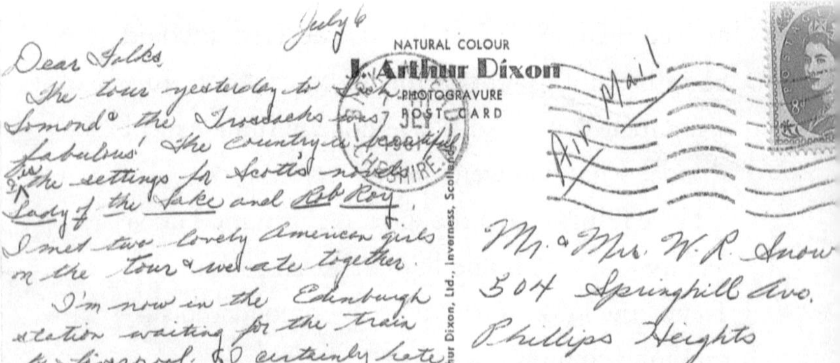

July 6

Dear Folks,
The tour yesterday to Loch Lomond & the Trossachs was fabulous! The country is beautiful – the settings for Scott's novels Lady of the Lake and Rob Roy.
I met two lovely American girls on the tour & we ate together.
I'm now in the Edinburgh station waiting for the train to Liverpool. I certainly hate to leave. This is one of the most charming & pittoresque (I don't remember Eng. sp.) towns I've seen! There are beautiful roses everywhere & a band stand in the middle of the park. I bought a little charm for my bracelet – a bag pipe.
Love, Bert

NATURAL COLOUR
J. Arthur Dixon
PHOTOGRAVURE
POST CARD

LOCH LOMOND AND BEN LOMOND,
from Luss, Dunbartonshire.
A Natural Colour Photograph

3415

Printed and Published by J. Arthur Dixon, Ltd., Inverness, Scotland

Air Mail!

Mr. & Mrs. W. R. Snow
504 Springhill Ave.
Phillips Heights
Wilmington 3, Delaware
U.S.A.

BY AIR MAIL
PAR AVION

July 6

Dear Folks,

The tour yesterday to Loch Lomand and the Trossachs was fabulous! The country is beautiful and is the setting for Scott's novels <u>Lady of the Lake</u> and <u>Rob Roy</u>. I met two lovely American girls on the tour and we ate together.

I'm now in the Edinburgh station waiting for the train to Liverpool. I certainly hate to leave. This is one of the most charming and pittoresque (I don't remember English sp.) towns I've seen!

There are beautiful roses everywhere and a bandstand in the middle of the park. I bought a little charm for my bracelet - a bagpipe.

Love, Barb

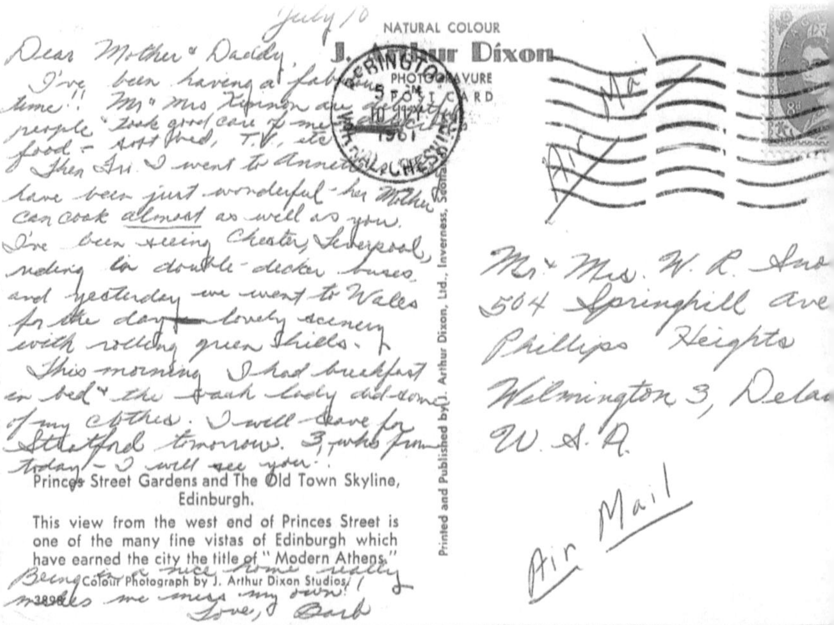

July 10

Dear Mother & Daddy,
I've been having a fabulous time. Mr & Mrs [Kenyon] are such nice people. Took good care of me - nice [room], food - rest [med], T.V. etc.
Then [Sat] I went to Anne's [and we] have been just wonderful - her Mother can cook almost as well as you.
I've been seeing Chester, Liverpool, riding in double-decker buses, and yesterday we went to Wales for the day - lovely scenery with rolling green hills.
This morning I had breakfast in bed & the bath lady did some of my clothes. I will leave for Stratford tomorrow. 3 [weeks from] today - I will see you.
Being [nice] to [me] [really]
[makes] me miss my own!
Love, Barb

Princes Street Gardens and The Old Town Skyline, Edinburgh.
This view from the west end of Princes Street is one of the many fine vistas of Edinburgh which have earned the city the title of "Modern Athens."
Colour Photograph by J. Arthur Dixon Studios.

Mr & Mrs. W. R. [Ano]
504 Springhill Ave
Phillips Heights
Wilmington 3, Dela[ware]
U. S. A.

Air Mail

July 10

Dear Mother & Daddy,

I've been having a fabulous time! Mr. & Mrs. Kinnon are delightful people and took good care of me - delicious food - soft bed, TV, etc.

Then Friday I went to Annette's. They have been just wonderful. Her mother can cook <u>almost</u> as well as you. I've been seeing Chester, Liverpool, riding in double-decker buses, and yesterday we went to Wales for the day - lovely scenery with rolling green hills.

This morning I had breakfast in bed and the wash lady did some of my clothes. I will leave for Stratford tomorrow. 3 weeks from today - I will see you!!

Being in a nice home really makes me miss my own!

Love, Barb

SHAKESPEARE'S BIRTHPLACE, STRATFORD-UPON-AVON

(Annette's parents)

Dear Folks,

I have arrived in Stratford after a grand time at Annette's. The scenery here is beautiful. I took a boat ride down the Avon.

Tickets are hard to get, but I found one for standing room. They are playing *Hamlet* tonight. Tomorrow morning I shall take a walk out to Anne Hathaway's Cottage & then take the bus to London.

I'm getting anxious to hear more news from you.
Mr. & Mrs. T. Henry
25 Higher Bebington Rd. Love,
Bebington
Wirral, Cheshire, England

Mr. & Mrs. W. R. Snow
504 Springhill Ave
Phillips Heights
Wilmington 3, Delaware
U.S.A.

Air Mail

July 11

Dear Folks,

I have arrived in Stratford after a grand time at Annette's. The scenery here is beautiful. I took a boat ride down the Avon.

Tickets are hard to get, but I found one for standing room! They are playing <u>Hamlet</u> tonight.

Tomorrow morning I shall take a walk out to Anne Hathaway's cottage and then take the bus to London.

I'm getting anxious to hear more news from you. Love, me

ST. PAUL'S CATHEDRAL, LONDON.

July 14

Dear Folks,

I'm back in London having a fabulous time! My landlady is delightful and wants me to go to mass with her Sun. and then to an outing at some park. I shall go to my church at night.

This morning I took a tour – saw London Tower – very interesting built by Wm. The Conqueror and also saw the crown jewels which left me cold!! I guess I've never learned to appreciate huge jewels on crowns.

This afternoon on my third try, I saw Yuri Gagarin. He is small, very cute, and has a lovely personality. Unfortunately, I was not presented to him. I was one of the crowd.

Love, me

July 17

Dear Mother & Daddy,

Well two weeks from today I should be seeing you!! Hope you are gathering in the food!! I met Glady the other night when she arrived. It was so good to see her. We talked for hours. Last night I took her to church and they invited us again for sandwiches and coffee afterwards.

Also met Ian Kinnon – very nice young man - he is huge. He took me to Petticoat Lane, then to a pub, then to dinner, and finally we walked thru the parks and went rowing on the Serpentine in Hyde Park.

Love, me

July 19

Dear Mother & Daddy,

I am having a delightful time! I sightsee during the day and go out with Ian at night. Also have seen Glady three times.

There seems to be some confusion according to yours and Roberta's letters as to my plans. I am going to Paris tomorrow. I get on the ship at Le Havre on the 26th at night. We leave the 27th. I'm not yet sure when we get in, but I think it's the morning of the 31st. At any rate, you can check a N. York paper or call a travel bureau. I will let you know my cabin number when I find out. Love, Barb

PS - if my trunk hasn't arrived, you can drive up in my car - maybe we can find it.

Goodbye To France

See you in a week!! You better be there!

July 24

Dear Folks,

I saw this Palace on an excursion yesterday. The "N" stands for Napoleon.

I'm having a marvelous time and thanks so much for the money. I was afraid I would not have any for the boat trip home! - tips, etc.

Glady arrived last night, and I took her to see the Eiffel Tower. We went up in it and looked down to see all the monuments lighted up. It is hard to express how beautiful it really is!

Tonight we're going to the Lido! I can hardly wait!

The plans for tomorrow are to take a boat ride along the Seine, visit the Louvre, see the Left Bank & Latin Quarter which I know the best (having gone to classes here) and then in the evening to see <u>Les Femmes Savantes</u> of Molière (my favorite author). I only wish you both could be here too.

Love, Barb

Length 990 ft.   S.S. UNITED STATES   Gr. tons 53,300
Largest, most luxurious ship ever built in America—the world's fastest liner, she established new trans-atlantic speed records eastbound and westbound on her maiden voyage. This flagship of the United States Lines and her running mate, the beautiful S.S. America operate in regular service between New York and Europe. United States Lines also operates 53 fast modern cargo ships in regular service between East Coast ports of the U.S.A. and Europe, Hawaii, Far East, Australia and New Zealand.

1961

"RICHKROME": EXCLUSIVELY BY STEELOGRAPH CO., ONE BROADWAY, NEW YORK   MADE IN U.S.A.

POST CARD

PLACE STAMP HERE

ADDRESS

Epilogue

UPON HER RETURN to Delaware, Barbara started teaching French at Stanton Middle School in Wilmington, Delaware. She taught there for four years. In September 1962, she met Paul Zitlau, a California transplant who worked for the DuPont company and rented an apartment in the same boarding house. They were engaged on Valentine's Day 1963 and were married in Newark, Delaware on June 22, 1963.

Two children followed: Kimberley in 1965 and Warren, named after her father, in 1968.

Due to the changes in her life and new responsibilities, Barbara lost touch with many of the people mentioned, except for her relatives and some childhood friends.

Her spiritual life took a notable turn after living in Nashville in 1969-1971. Upon the Zitlaus' return to Delaware, they left the Presbyterian Church (USA) and joined the Reformed Presbyterian Church Evangelical Synod, which merged with the Presbyterian Church of America (PCA) in 1982. She was active in her church, the Evangelical Presbyterian Church of Newark, Delaware, until her declining health precipitated a move to Maryland in 2014. In that church community Barbara met her lifelong friend and sister, Joan Lazeration.

Barbara did not travel much internationally, but the world came to her. She and her husband Paul served as a host family to foreign graduate students at the University of Delaware. She helped these students navigate a new culture and foreign bureaucracy like she had as a young woman abroad. She also provided home-cooked meals and emotional support. These acts of service stemmed from her faith and were a connection to her French and Spanish adventures decades earlier.

Some young women became like adopted daughters: Emma from France, Ana from Spain, and Yuri from Japan.

She only returned to Europe once to attend the wedding of her Spanish daughter Ana in 2000. During that trip she revisited Madrid, Toledo, and Granada, as well as new cities, Jaén and Jódar.

After succumbing to the effects of dementia, Barbara died in November 2017. Her faith, laughter, and loving concern made her a blessing to many. Her final resting place is in All Saints Cemetery in Wilmington, Delaware.

Barbara on the evening celebrating her 50th wedding anniversary

www.ingramcontent.com/pod-product-compliance
Lightning Source LLC
Chambersburg PA
CBHW022041200426
43209CB00072B/1915/J